The Business Wealth Builders

The Business Wealth Builders

Accelerating Business Growth,
Maximizing Profits,
and Creating Wealth

Phil Symchych
Alan Weiss

BUSINESS EXPERT PRESS

The Business Wealth Builders: Accelerating Business Growth, Maximizing Profits, and Creating Wealth

First published in 2016 by
Business Expert Press, LLC
222 East 46th Street, New York, NY 10017
www.businessexpertpress.com

ISBN-13: 978-1-63157-290-6 (paperback)
ISBN-13: 978-1-63157-291-3 (e-book)

Business Expert Press Entrepreneurship and Small Business Management Collection

Collection ISSN: 1946-5653 (print)
Collection ISSN: 1946-5661 (electronic)

Cover and interior design by S4Carlisle Publishing Services Private Ltd., Chennai, India

First edition: 2016

10 9 8 7 6 5 4 3 2 1

Printed in the United States of America.

Dedication

To Phil's wife, Kerry Ottenbreit, and daughters, Anastasia and Julia. Thank you for making life much more rewarding, interesting, and fun.

To Alan's grandchildren, Alaina and Gabrielle, may they grow up in a peaceful and prosperous world.

To business owners around the world, who drive our economies, innovate, take risks, employ people, and provide us with the highest standard of living that we often take for granted.

Abstract

The Business Wealth Builders provides pragmatic advice for business owners of privately held, small and medium enterprises (SMEs) on how to grow their businesses, increase top-line revenues and bottom-line profits, enhance the value of their companies, and build their business wealth. This book is written for business owners, managers, executives, family business members, business advisors such as accountants and bankers, industry and trade associations, entrepreneurs, and students and professors of entrepreneurship and business. SMEs drive half of the economy in North America and generate the majority of net new jobs, so their performance and contributions to our standard of living are critically important. As large companies downsize, rightsize, offshore, and onshore their operations, entrepreneurs are innovating, hiring, and growing their businesses. Readers will benefit by learning techniques to sharpen their strategies, attract and retain more customers, deliver better products and services more quickly, charge higher prices, increase profits, and create businesses that are more valuable, more saleable, and more attractive to future owners, employees, and customers.

Keywords

How to grow your business, Business funding, Business financing, Business growth, Business capital, Business growth strategies, Business owner, Entrepreneur, Profit, Business value, Business equity, Wealth builder, Wealth building, Succession plan, Family business

Contents

Acknowledgments

Thanks to my first business mentors: my parents, John and Phyllis Symchych, and Uncle Peter and Aunt Norma Drosdowech, who purchased and operated Clear Lake Lodge for almost two decades. We learned a lot when interest rates were 20 percent.

This book would never have happened if not for the supreme mentoring and years of wise advice from my mentor and friend, Alan Weiss. Alan, the wisdom you share, from technical consulting, to marketing, to how to live life to its fullest, is priceless.

I extend gratitude, respect and appreciation to all clients, especially: Ewen and Shirley Morrison, Dale and Teresa Hensrud, Donna Dynna, Doug and Gloria Archer, James Archer, Tracy Rogoza, Garnet Bjornerud, Dave and Denise Peter, Wayne Morsky, Lorne Schnell, Gilbert Chan, Frank and Lana Shewchuk, Randy, Jason, Colin and Brock Hrywkiw, and all of my business clients and SME Advisors. You have all contributed to the ideas in this book.

I've worked closely with many excellent accountants, lawyers, and bankers who proactively help their clients, including Doug Yaremko, Lon Sokalski, Jeff Pietrobon, Ron Boychuk, Stuart Pollon, Dave Kowalishen, and my trusted advisor, Kelly Ozem.

Phil Symchych

I'd like to acknowledge my global mentoring and coaching communities which serve as both my laboratory and motivational fuel. And I thank my coauthor, Phil, for this opportunity to learn so much about small businesses.

Alan Weiss

Disclaimer

Every business situation is unique. We recommend that you obtain professional advice regarding all technical matters including, but not limited to, accounting, tax, legal, and other information. We accept no responsibility for the outcomes of any actions taken as a result of the information in this book.

Introduction

Closely held business hiring comprises almost 100 percent of the net new jobs created in the United States annually, according to the Bureau of Labor Statistics. Fortune 1000 firms replace jobs but do not create new ones, thanks to technology, outsourcing, off-shoring, and cost reductions.

Hence, what we colloquially call "small business" (which can easily be in the hundreds of millions in revenue) are the economic generators of the country. Not many people realize that, including people who own these businesses. They are often neglected in the media, in investment, in development, and in public appreciation.

This book is intended for the owners of those firms, who deserve to be rewarded more handsomely, gain more recognition for their entrepreneurialism, and sleep more soundly knowing their wealth is protected and legacy intact.

We have the rather distinct backgrounds of having consulted with top Fortune 1000 companies globally, with closely held businesses through North America—from about $2 million to $200 million in revenues—and are the owners of small businesses ourselves for several decades. We think those frames of reference provide us with some unique value to offer in terms of best practices and pragmatic advice.

We deeply respect the intricacy of managing family issues and business needs that are so often inextricably woven together in these business segments. We acknowledge the need for the intellectual decision alongside the emotional realities in such environments.

What we've tried to provide—and hope you find—is the most direct and fastest path to a highly profitable business and extremely rewarding life, with options along the way to ensure the proper mid-course corrections.

They may call it "small business," but it's of large import.

Phil Symchych, Regina, Saskatchewan
Alan Weiss, East Greenwich, Rhode Island
June 1, 2015

PART 1

The Big Impact of Small Business

CHAPTER 1

Mindset: It's not Personal, it's Business, or is it?

Is your name on the sign? Are you the founder, successor, or majority shareholder? Does your personal wealth and future depend on the success of your business?

Just like Cargill, Ford, or Hewlett Packard, many great companies have succeeded beyond their founder's greatest expectations by following the same path that you and your business are on today. Maybe you are one of today's high-growth successful companies like EMW Industrial, Knight Archer, or McKenna Distribution with futures that are limited only by the energy and enthusiasm of their owners and managers. In today's dynamic global environment, the most critical growth factor is your mindset. (I worked with a $1.2-billion construction firm in Detroit that was begun as—and still retained—subchapter S legal status!)

Your mindset drives your business in pursuit of success. In school, our teachers taught us that there is usually one correct answer. In business, there is seldom a single right answer. In fact, you have likely experienced two outcomes to your business decisions and actions: either "that worked and we should have done it sooner" or "that didn't work but let's learn from it and move on." The first outcome is about *speed* and the second outcome is about *leverage*. Combining speed and leverage is optimal for growing your revenues, profits, valuation, and wealth.

Our main premise is that your wealth is tied to your earnings, and more specifically, your EBITDA (earnings before interest, taxes, depreciation, and amortization). Therefore, maximizing earnings will maximize your wealth. Many businesses may be able to increase their EBITDA without growing top-line revenues. Other businesses can increase their valuation without any growth at all and we'll discuss these options in later chapters.

The Meek Shall Not Inherit the Earth: It's About Speed and Leverage

Meekness is not a viable business strategy! You're competing with companies across the street and around the world. The faster that you can respond to your prospect's or customer's request, the more likely that you will win the business. If you can leverage both your customer relationships and your production capacity, you can quickly grow your business and build your wealth. If you can't, well, your competitor probably can. Zappos and Amazon have shown us how this is done on a large scale, but myriad numbers of auto parts stores, beauty salons, dry cleaners, and clothing stores are engaged in speed and leverage daily, as are your own direct competitors.

Speed

Today's cars are capable of driving double the speed limit in many places and some that are designed for Europe's unlimited highways can go even faster. Yet, speed limits are the rule and are put in place to protect everyone from acting rashly and to control the roads.

But there are no speed limits in business. Speed depends on you.

Take this speed test to determine how quickly you can grow your business. Low means it takes most of a year; medium means within 90 days; and high means this week (Table 1.1).

Your growth speed will be limited by the slowest variable in the table below. If you go faster than the slowest variable, it can be very dangerous to your business and your wealth. What's the safe rate of acceleration to increase your sales and production without running out of fuel, that is, cash?

Table 1.1 Speed test

How quickly can you:	Low	Med	High
Increase sales			
Increase production			
Fund your growth with cash or debt			
Provide information on the above factors			

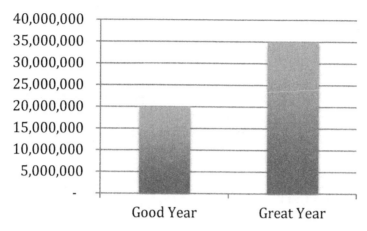

Figure 1.1 **EMW revenue growth**

EMW Industrial grew from $20 million to $35 million in one year. That 75 percent revenue growth was achieved because of management's ability to implement pricing strategies, attract and retain talent, control larger projects, and obtain their banker's support in funding that growth (Figure 1.1).

Your business is an organic entity that wants to grow. Many midmarket companies have the Fortune 500 as their best customers. As the major corporations focus on their core competence and outsource the back office and everything else, that creates significant growth opportunities for midmarket companies. However, the big companies need you to deliver massive quantities on time and on budget.

To do that, you need to scale up. You need to think like a larger company while preserving your strengths of speed, flexibility, and customer responsiveness.

Race cars are extreme because they're powerful, aerodynamic, and driven by slightly crazy people who like to go really fast. There's also a pit crew and management team monitoring all of the car's conditions in real time. Your business is like a race car because you can use power (cash), aerodynamics (information), and good management to accelerate to top speed (Figure 1.2).

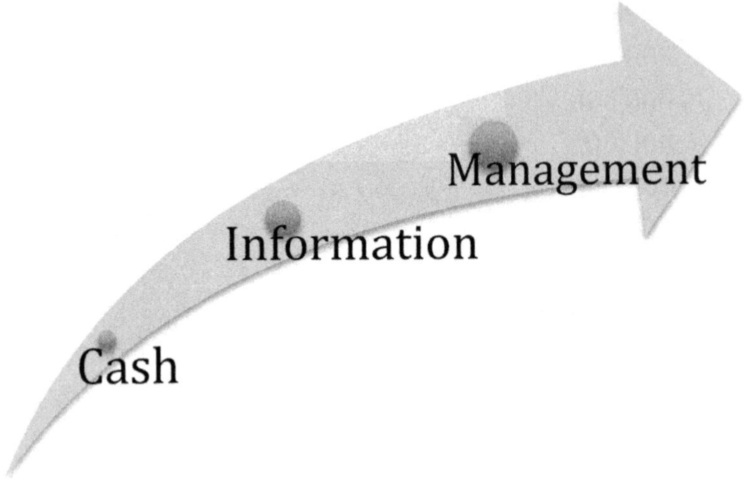

Management

Information

Cash

Figure 1.2 Business growth accelerators

Businesses can accelerate their growth by doing three things. First, they can add power with strong cash flow that fuels continued acceleration. A highly profitable business can fund its own growth. Most businesses in growth mode will need external funding. If you want to build your wealth, you need to pull money out of your company as it continues to grow so financing makes lots of sense (more about that later).

Second, businesses can improve their aerodynamics by reducing their drag on profits and shutting down their low-margin products and services. Every business has winners and losers. At the time of this writing, Apple recently had a record quarter in terms of revenues and profits from sales of a new iPhone model (37,000 sold *every hour* for 90 days!). This model cannibalized sales of its older models but generated higher revenues and profits than its competitors, Samsung and RIM, who were slower to release new products. Are you cannibalizing your own products? Are you at least stopping the money losers?

Case Study: Speed and Leverage

The first bars to offer "happy hour" in a neighborhood with inexpensive food and drinks (or "ladies' night" or whatever) not only draw the largest crowds of the competition, but also retain those crowds even after the competition copies the offer.

Finally, giving your management team access to real-time information so that they can make better decisions, faster will accelerate your growth. The most critical piece of information isn't financial as those are usually lag indicators (meaning they're not "real time" and don't aid in speed), it's your production numbers: How much did you produce *today?* Rick Pay, an operations expert in Portland, advises his clients to focus on "Shipped On Time." If you can't produce it and ship it, you can't sell it.

Therefore, successful, high-growth companies that create strong profits and build wealth for their stakeholders utilize three common factors to achieve speed and leverage: management, information, and cash.

What is your main growth barrier: marketing, production, or cash? Identifying the key barrier and resolving it will accelerate your growth. As you resolve one barrier, one of the other factors will become the new barrier. As Eli Goldratt observed in his book, *The Goal*, it's normal to see new bottlenecks appear in production as you resolve other bottlenecks.

Leverage can be internal or external. An example of internal leverage is to identify internal best practices and share those throughout your company. Car dealers, who spend millions advertising to get new customers in the door, do this very well. The most profitable car dealerships focus on problems such as when a customer has a breakdown and then they go out of their way to help the customer.

> **Wealth Building Blocks:** "Best practices" are normally best found *internally*, not outside your business. Identify what you're doing well in some places, and make sure it's done well in all places.

I was driving to an important board meeting two hours away when I heard the unmistakable gloom of a flat tire. I called (hands-free) the dealership (while still driving on run-flat tires) and requested a tire repair. The dealer, Dilawri BMW, didn't fix my tire right away as this would have made me late for the meeting; instead, provided another vehicle while they took care of my car.

That kind of proactive approach to solving a customer's problem creates significant leverage with the customer. It increases loyalty, referrals, and repeat business. This story is in newsletters, in speeches, and now, in this book. That's excellent leverage for Andy Kistener and his great team at Dilawri.

Industry trade associations could immediately improve their value by helping their members share best practices. They have members of various levels of success. Many members may see each other as competitors and reluctant to share information or best practices. If the individual businesses don't share and become stronger, then large corporate entities with national or international scale will either acquire the smaller ones or just step on them and squish them.

Another example of external leverage is outsourcing. A manufacturer of mobile storage units doubled production by outsourcing part of the manufacturing process to a much larger and more sophisticated manufacturer who specialized in their subcomponents. They doubled production without any capital investment. That accomplished both speed and leverage. To increase your external leverage, answer these questions:

- What companies do what you do on a larger scale?
- What can you learn from them?
- How can you utilize them to grow your business and build your wealth?

Speed and leverage are about the execution of your business strategy. An average strategy that is executed quickly will trump a great strategy that is executed poorly. Full speed ahead!

Business is sport: Playing to Win vs. Playing Not to Lose

You need offense to score points and win games; defense alone usually doesn't score points or win games. It's the same in business except you've got more than one competitor and the playing field is definitely not level. The trick is to make it uneven in your favor!

You have global competitors with lower labor costs and lower overheads that are causing price pressure. You have invisible competitors such as high-growth and niche companies which aren't on your radar yet but which are already calling on your customers. You have innovative competitors who aren't tied to your legacy products and whose egos aren't stuck in doing things a certain way (Figure 1.3).

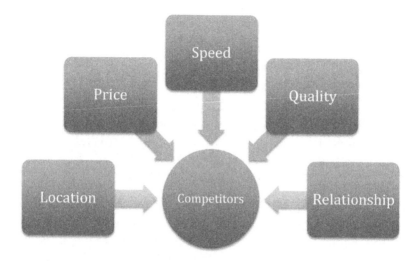

Figure 1.3 Competitive factors

Your competitors are playing to win. They're hungry and aggressive. These are the same factors that helped you turn your small business into a midmarket company. These factors turned new ideas into major successes for many Fortune 500 companies, such as Apple.

The 2015 Super Bowl preliminaries featured the Green Bay Packers losing the conference championship to the Seattle Seahawks, largely because Green Bay played "not to lose" and gave up a significant lead to the Seahawks, who came from behind to win in the last three minutes of the game after trailing badly and playing poorly. You have to play all 60 minutes. The Patriots won the Super Bowl over the Seahawks on the last meaningful play of the game with 20 seconds left.

The USA men's basketball team has won a medal at almost every summer Olympics where basketball has been played since 1936, 17 medals in all, including 14 gold, 1 silver, and 2 bronze. They don't just play to win, they play to win the gold. They know they're the best players in the world. Their confidence drives their success.

The Patriots don't play to make the play-offs or to have a winning record. They play to *win the Super Bowl every year,* and have won an astonishing four in 13 years, having played in six over that span.

Businesses need more confidence and clarity so that they know what they're really good at and they can play to win. It's not just about methodology or processes, but, more importantly, *it's about the economic results and emotional value that they create for customers and clients.* If they can't articulate their results and value, then they end up competing on price, and that is a race to the bottom all to easily won.

> **Wealth Building Blocks:** You're not in business to avoid loss or to maintain the status quo. You're in business to *grow.* You're not here to stick a tow in the water. You're here to make waves.

Businesses can turn commodities that characteristically have intense price competition and few differentiators into high-value offerings by enhancing the other factors around the commodity acquisition and installation, including ordering, payment, storage, maintenance, monitoring, financing, and even ownership. Every company has an internal cost of time, people, and money to acquire something. You can never make it too easy or too much fun for a company to do business with you. *Key question*: What can you do to make it easier and more fun for your best customers to do more business with you?

> **Case Study: Providence Apple Store**
>
> I walked in having lost my iPad and needing a new one quickly. A greeter at the door said, whimsically, "We have iPads!" and showed me the models. I knew what I wanted, he punched it in on his phone, and said it would take just a couple of minutes. In about a minute a guy walked over from the back with an iPad and cover.
>
> The transaction was completed right there with my credit card and a receipt was sent to me electronically.
>
> *The entire sale had taken less than eight minutes, and I had never been more than six feet into the store.* When I called my wife on my phone to say I was ready to leave, she couldn't believe it, she had barely found the store she wanted.

When competitors launch new offerings, many established businesses either ignore the competitor or underestimate the market's response for a new offering. There are several causes: from human nature's natural tendency for denial (as part of a grieving process or to protect the psyche in times of stress or threat), to a short-term focus on operations, to attachment on their own plans to support their ego. This has resulted in massive business failures, including Radio Shack, RIM/Blackberry, Kodak, and Polaroid, and probably two dozen shops on the nearest "Main Street" to your home.

Playing to win means that you need to keep score. Even as kids playing stick ball or street hockey, we kept score. Businesses can improve performance dramatically by measuring key sales and productivity results, posting the results and holding people accountable for performance (Figure 1.4).

Do you have the proper metrics in place (see figure below) to effectively "keep score," and determine whether you're winning, losing, or tied? Are you checking them every day? That's right: every day.

The purpose of your business isn't to have a happy employee, although they will perform better when they're happy; the purpose is to take care of your customer. Your customers vote with their wallets. If you can't demonstrate a high ROI for your customer, they will buy from someone else. If your customer buys from someone else, you don't get a silver medal for losing to a competitor who got the gold, literally. You get nothing.

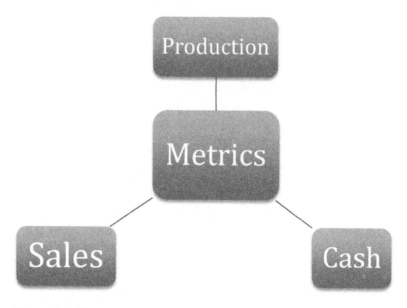

Figure 1.4 Key metrics for business performance

The key points to playing to win and knowing the score are the following:

- Make sure that you know the *real* score. You need to quantify the results that you create for your customers in terms of economic results such as revenue growth, cost savings, or productivity and efficiency gains. You need to measure the emotional value of increased confidence, reduced stress, time saved, promotions received, and brands strengthened.
- Compete at both the logical and the emotional levels so that you can clearly differentiate yourself from your competitors. Logic makes people think, but emotion makes them act. Are your employees making emotional connections with your buyers?
- Play to win by aggressively going after new business and building strong relationships with your customers so they perceive you as a strategic partner who is proactively helping them increase their success. Don't focus on trying "not to lose" business. Focus on expanding and gaining business.
- Celebrate your successes. Learn from them and replicate them. Embrace your employees and customers in celebrating success (parties, discounts, free value, coupons, and so forth).
- Cut the losers in terms of poor offerings and poor performers so that you can increase resources for the winners. You can't reach out if you don't let go.
- The fastest way to victory is to build on your strengths and successes. Don't focus on "postmortems." Focus on "postvictories."

Self-Esteem and Self-Confidence: The True Business Drivers

The business of success and the success of business are rooted in the art and science of psychology. That's because we're all people interacting with other people and *every* business is about communications and influence.

When the butcher, or tailor, or store owner greets you by name and knows your preferences, you're seeing the power of communications and influence at work in small business environments.

Here are some definitions to frame our discussion. Consider that self-esteem is really a verb or action that empowers you to create the condition of self-confidence, a noun. As your self-esteem becomes stronger, your self-confidence will grow. As your self-confidence grows, you will appreciate your own worth, both personally and professionally, and be more self-assured in asking to be compensated for your value. That's right, self-esteem drives pricing and accelerates the creation of wealth, as shown in Figure 1.5.

As physical exercise is necessary on a regular basis to maintain muscle tone, stamina, and health, self-esteem requires daily attention and constant reinforcement. When a customer berates you for a real or imagined sleight, you must be in a position to provide the correct perspective and response (e.g., apology, refund, listening, refusal, rebuttal—the customer is not always right).

When I first started consulting, I thought that most small and medium businesses lacked working capital. I was wrong about that being the key issue. It turned out that many business owners lacked self-esteem. These self-esteem problems caused, indirectly and directly, the lack of working capital.

The cause of low self-esteem among business owners is that too many take their customers' and prospects' criticisms personally. If a customer complains about your price but still does business with you and comes back for more, they're really not unhappy with your price. A great strategy

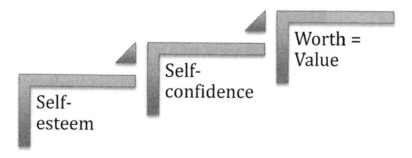

Figure 1.5 The psychological steps of building worth and wealth

to follow is like a quarterback who throws an interception or a goalie who lets in a goal: they just shake it off and get ready for the next play. Tom Brady, the Patriots' quarterback, threw two interceptions in the Super Bowl before leading the team on its winning drive with just a few minutes to play.

I mentioned pricing here because it's the ultimate demonstration of your self-esteem and self-confidence. If you believe your product is average, or worse, then you won't push your customers for premium pricing. If you provide a commodity product or service, then your customer will use easily available information on competitors' prices to negotiate more favorable terms.

Case Study:
Some time ago, a study was done of advertising firms to determine what their customers thought of them compared to what they thought of themselves. Astonishingly, the customers were far more delighted with the firms' results than the firms themselves were, and generally held a higher opinion of the ad firms' abilities than the ad firms held of themselves.

Wealth Building Blocks: Think about the repercussions in terms of bending to client demands, pricing, innovation, risk taking, and so forth. A lack of self-esteem was undermining profitability considerably.

Although it may be difficult to be objective of criticism from a customer, especially when your name is on the front door, often the criticisms are poorly disguised negotiation strategies in order to obtain lower prices or additional benefits. The customer wants you to think that their business is at risk so that you'll lower your price to retain them. The customer is using emotional leverage against you because they know you need to meet payroll and keep your business afloat.

This happens more frequently when larger companies negotiate with smaller, privately held businesses. In fact, large companies have taken this art of negotiation and turned it into a science called procurement.

However, it's a phenomenon across organizational life. The vaunted ability of a Ritz-Carlton employee to spend up to $2,500 without approval to comfort an unhappy guest ("We are ladies and gentlemen servicing ladies and gentlemen") has quietly been deemphasized in the aftermath of Marriott buying the chain. Too many Ritz-Carlton employees were offering a free night when a free drink—or even merely an apology—would have sufficed.

Do you identify yourself with what you do? Are you a business owner, entrepreneur, architect, mechanic, or creator? Do you fix things or make things? The major problem with identifying with our professions or skills is that it limits our ability to see the full impact and value of our contributions. This self-limiting label negatively impacts our self-esteem.

One company owner said, "We fix things when they break." He focused on his mechanical training and what his company did for his customers. As a result, he seriously underestimated his own value. Do teachers present a lesson plan, or do they build future citizens? Do bus drivers steer a bus, or deliver people safely and on time for personal and work needs? Does an insurance agent sell policies or provide families with peace of mind?

Which of my alternatives are worth more?

When the owner focused externally on the customer and how the customer benefited, he discovered a huge impact that he wasn't previously aware of from his own perspective. The company's expertise and knowledge helped his customers to allocate time and money in very beneficial ways. His services helped his customers to keep their equipment running, increase revenues and maximize the useful life of their assets.

The owner shifted his strategy from being a reactive fixer to a proactive maximizer of machine uptime, revenues, and asset life. His customers loved his new focus and responded positively to his presentations. The owner doubled his fees, dramatically increased his profits and grew his business over 400 percent.

Wealth Building Blocks: Is your emphasis on your input or output, on your deliverable or your result? What have you instilled in your employees? Self-esteem means believing in the value of your contributions, not the time you spend during the day.

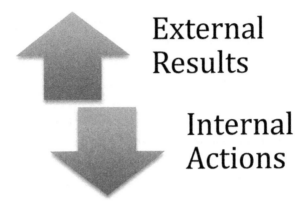

Figure 1.6 The strategic value of focusing on external results.

Key Questions:

How are you communicating your value and educating your customers? Are you focusing on external results or internal activities (Figure 1.6)?

Self-esteem impacts strategy, as shown in the diagram above. When a business focuses on—and quantifies and communicates—the powerful results they create for their clients, such as increased profits or attracting new customers, this increases customer attraction and empowers premium pricing. If a business just talks about what they do—their inputs— then the customer is left to compare this provider to all other similar providers, which is a pricing decision. You know what happens next: Due to lots of competitors for a perceived commodity, prices start an ugly tumble to the bottom.

The keys to positive self-esteem are in recognizing what your contributions and outcomes are, and how valuable they are to others. You need to apply the proper "self-talk" to ensure you're building that power daily.[1]

The main steps in improving your self-esteem and increasing your self-confidence so that you can build your business wealth are the following:

1. Quantify the results that you've created for your best customers. This includes revenues and profits created, costs saved, customers attracted, and intangible factors such as increased brand recognition, more engaged employees, and a positive culture.

---

[1]See *Learned Optimism* by Dr. Martin Seligman for the best discussion of the elements and discipline of positive self-talk.

2. Ask your best customers to describe the long-term impact and results that you've created for them. Record these on video and audio and use the testimonials to attract new customers.

3. Reflect on your unique value, the obstacles that you've overcome and the successes that you've achieved. Use these positive accomplishments to create confident messages for yourself, your team, and your customers.

You can only replicate success if you understand the *causes* of that success. These questions will help you to constantly be working on the improvement and sustainment of high self-esteem for you, your employees, and your business.

Getting in Shape: Why You're More Valuable than a Multimillion Dollar Athlete

Most midsize business owners are more valuable than the multimillion dollar athletes that they follow on television because of the business impact on employees and suppliers, yet the owners' physical condition may not align with their economic power or importance. Many owners sacrifice their health for their business until a health crisis changes their course and their business.

Donna Dynna was enjoying semiretirement while still working part-time at MuniSoft, the software company her husband Glenn and she founded three decades ago. Life was good and she was cruising into retirement. Then, the unthinkable happened, and Glenn fell off a ladder while removing snow from the roof of their sun room. He fell into a coma and passed away from his injuries. Donna, a grieving widow, was thrust back into a leadership position at MuniSoft. Her business health was in jeopardy and its future was up to her.

Donna sought external help as she considered her options: She could sell the company as is, hire someone to run the specialized software company, or take control and plan the future. She chose the last, promoted a key employee to be the general manager, and built a management team around her new position of president. Over the next couple of years she visited her major customers on her summer tours, developed and launched new products, expanded services to include training, and generated record revenues. Her son, Mark Dynna, an engineer by training, is being groomed to become the president and take over the company.

In her role as president, she improved the health of her business and has succeeded at being semi-retired. Now, she works "T to T, T to T" as she likes to say, which means that she works Tuesday to Thursday, ten in the morning to three in the afternoon. MuniSoft's management team runs the business on a day-to-day basis and Donna, as the president, guides the overall direction.

Business Health Factors

How healthy is your business according to these factors (Figure 1.7):

1. The owner can step out of the business for several months and the business will continue to operate and grow profitably.
2. The business has clear succession plans for all key leaders.
3. Future strategies are in place to strengthen the company's position with new products and services.
4. Relationships with key customers and prospects are being nurtured proactively.
5. Employee skills are continually being enhanced to make them more engaged and productive.

Figure 1.7 Business health factors

I define wealth as discretionary time. Therefore, our objective is to increase your wealth and provide you with more freedom from your business. Otherwise, the blind pursuit of money and disregard for your health will erode your wealth.

Donna didn't just get her business into shape, she got herself into the best shape of her life. She joined Level 10, a local gym owned by Dan Farthing, a former Saskatchewan Roughrider receiver in the Canadian Football League. She hired Alyssa Herman as her personal trainer and has worked out with her twice per week. She hired a nutrition coach who created an easy to follow meal plan. As a result, Donna lost 30 pounds, dropped three dress sizes, and earned the nickname "Hot Donna" (from "That 70's Show") from her trainers at the gym.

The number one indicator of health risk is waist circumference. An article on Harvard's School of Public Health website (http://www.hsph. harvard.edu/obesity-prevention-source/obesity-definition/abdominal-obesity/) called "Waist Size Matters" explains the results of different research studies on waist circumference. Women who carried extra weight around their waist rather than their hips and who had a waist of 35 inches or more had significantly increased risk of cardiovascular diseases and cancer compared to women whose waists were less than 35 inches.

Most men carry their extra weight on their waist and their health risks are the same for increased premature death from heart attacks, strokes, and cancer. Waist fat is bad because it also surrounds the internal organs, is metabolically active, and results in "higher LDL cholesterol, triglycerides, blood glucose, and blood pressure," according to the article.

Another major health risk for business owners is stress. Stress causes the release of cortisol and triggers the "fight or flight" response even though we aren't in physical danger running our businesses. When stress occurs, it is most important to identify and treat the cause of the stress rather than medicating the symptoms with drugs and alcohol.

Stress in corporate setting is often based on two factors:

1. I feel I don't know what will happen in the short-term future.
2. I feel I have no control over what might happen.

Obviously, for business owners, a sense of control is important and quite reasonable.

Key Questions

- Do you take better care of your car than you do of your own body?
- How are you reducing the causes of stress in your personal and professional life?
- What is your waist circumference?
- What is your plan to improve your health?

Your family, employees, customers, and suppliers are counting on you to be around for a long time. That length of time is up to you.

See our Personal Balance Sheet assessment in the Appendix to determine your profile, strengths, and risks.

How to Get a Life: Creating Your Ideal Business and Your Ideal Life

How do you define a successful life? If it's just about money, then you're merely a "collector." Some of the most boring people I know are focused solely on collecting money. I call this the "ker-ching moment" and the "turnstile mentality." They've burned up important relationships in their life. Their health is getting worse, not better. Their bank account is getting better so they think they're living the dream. But they've got the wrong metric. And if true wealth is discretionary time, then they're collecting money while eroding their wealth.

Money is important. All business owners know that money is fuel for the business and fuel for their personal lives. However, the most successful people that I advise don't focus just on creating more fuel, they create more life for themselves, their families, and their employees. Fuel is worthless unless it's propelling something.

So let's talk about you.

Can you take six weeks away from your business all at once and oversee operations remotely? Do you plan your vacations for the next year ahead or do you take holidays only if the extra time becomes available? Does your business dictate your personal schedule? Or, can you combine business and pleasure into one trip so you're maximizing both?

The purpose of your business is to provide you with fuel—time, energy, money, and fun (Figure 1.8)—so that you can enjoy your life. Every day can be like a working holiday where you contribute to your business and to your own life. How well does your business provide you with free time, increase your energy, fund your wealth, and make you happy each day?

Yet many business owners, especially during high-growth phases and the transition from being a small business to being a midsize business, are the primary fuel for their businesses. Since most of you reading this are already midsize business leaders, you've already learned to let go of tasks, delegate to others, and organize your team to pursue larger goals. You will be happiest and most productive when you are utilizing your natural talents and pursing the work that you are most passionate about. How well does your current role utilize your natural talents and passions?

Wealth Building Blocks: Strong leaders are surrounded by strong, trustworthy people. Weak leaders are surrounded by weak, nonaccountable people. These relationships never change.

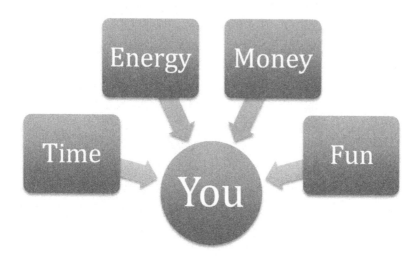

Figure 1.8 Business is fuel for your life

It may sound counterintuitive, but your business will really accelerate its growth rate when you focus on your ultimate utilization of your talents and passions. That combination or recipe is what is most unique about you and that can create a business that can't be replicated. Richard Branson is wildly successful because his businesses personify his passions. Many global companies like HP, Apple, and FedEx, got their start because their founders focused on utilizing their passions to pursue an opportunity. Ben and Jerry's Ice Cream ran this route growing to the point where it became an icon for small business success. When work is play, it stops being work, and that's a major step toward getting a life. Is going to work like going to play?

Many professions, such as firefighters, police, nurses, and teachers, attract people who are committed to helping other people. Yet the risk of burnout is high in some of these professions because the person isn't in control of the work, must deal with bureaucratic people and procedures, and can't control time. As an entrepreneur, you don't need to suffer any of those ills. You control the people, the processes, and the pace of workflow. Controlling your environment will reduce your stress and help you to get a life. Does your environment support you to be your best?

Some professionals such as university professors can take a six-month or longer sabbatical to recharge their personal and professional souls. I recommend that business owners take a weekly sabbatical so they are continually and optimally recharged and enjoying life every step of the way. Take an hour every Friday, or the entire afternoon on Wednesday, or whatever. When was your last sabbatical?

Are you working in your business or ON your business?

The purpose of this book is to build your wealth and continue to improve your life. I believe in instant gratification as that provides a maximum return on investment in terms of your time and energy. Here are 5 steps that you can take to create a great life.

1. Accept personal accountability for everything in your life (a good resource by Randy Gage: *Why you're sick, dumb and broke*).
2. Eliminate the stressors and negative influences in your life immediately and permanently; change relationships if you have to.

3. Never accept unsolicited advice as it's for the benefit of the giver, not you, and it may be even be malicious. Solicit advice from people whom you respect and even then look for patterns, not one-off suggestions.

4. Identify and throw your baggage off the train, even if it kills a few cows in the countryside. Everyone needs baggage, of course, but it should be baggage you pack for your immediate needs, not stuff given you 30 years ago and no longer vaguely relevant.

5. Develop and strengthen an abundance mentality where you have confidence in yourself to continually create wealth. This is the opposite of a poverty mentality that is rooted in fear. (An excellent reference on self-talk in this area: *Learned Optimism* by Dr. Martin Seligman.)

I'm on a ski trip as I write this chapter. It's one of my personal philosophies to continually learn and to "always hire an expert." So with that in mind, my family takes ski lessons in the morning. Our instructor, Vern Cole, retired as an engineer from a major oil company at the age of 51. For the last 18 years, he has focused on hunting, fishing, golf, and skiing. He offers ski lessons because he was bored with just skiing alone and now he gets to meet interesting people. Every day, he is doing something that he loves and helping others. Now that's a life.

The best way to leave a legacy is to live a great life. (For more information on how to build a great life, see *Thrive* by Dr. Alan Weiss.)

CHAPTER 2

Global Economic Power: The Massive (unappreciated) Momentum of the Small Business Entrepreneurs

Global Economic Significance: Driving 52 Percent of the GDP in the Top 17 Economies

Small and medium businesses drive our economies and our standard of living. In the United States, they provide the *majority* of net new jobs annually. (Large corporations hire only about as many as they lose, because they tend to improve productivity through technology.)

There are over five million small and medium businesses (defined as having two to 500 employees) in the United States and just under one million in Canada (note: we excluded sole proprietors from our statistics). In the United States, small businesses account for 63 percent of the net new jobs created with firms in the 20 to 499 employees category, leading to job creation. Small businesses employ 48.5 percent *of the total private sector employment*, according to the Small Business Administration's 2014 report.

Globally, the World Bank states that SMEs[1] (with up to 250 employees) contribute 52 percent of the Gross Domestic Product (GDP) in the top 17 economies. If we expand the World Bank's criteria to include companies with up to 500 employees, the economic impact is even more significant.

SMEs account for 33 percent of total export value in the United States and 25 percent of the value in Canada.

---

[1]Small and medium enterprises.

Our standard of living is driven, in large part, by overall employment levels, and closely held businesses are the winners in creating new jobs. Travel and technology have turned every business owner into a potential global superstar. Everyone with a smart phone is a potential customer. Bear in mind that China has about 1.4 billion people, India about 1.2, and the continent of Africa about 1.1. Most of these people will be accessible to most small businesses via technology in the next several years.

The recent 2008 financial crisis showed the world that the actions of a few can cause harm to many. Since the economy is critical to our standard of living, what can and should small business owners do to strengthen their enterprises?

The main factors affecting business growth and wealth creation for owners are external economic conditions, including financing, access to labor, technology to improve productivity, and taxes (Figure 2.1).

The World Bank states that the number one factor holding firms back from growth is the lack of access to capital. When small business owners are first starting their businesses and apply for business loans, the bankers base those business loans on the owner's personal credit history and personal net worth. Established business owners, the main beneficiaries of this book, have an easier time raising capital than new business owners, but not by much.

Wealth Building Blocks: Net worth is critical, and the capability of self-financing is a key factor in net worth.

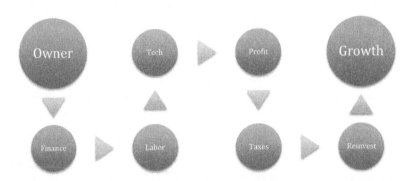

Figure 2.1 Economic growth factors

Fortunately, the North American banking environment is getting more stable and more competitive. However, banks are really just renters of money and they prefer to hold security to protect their money. The 2008 financial crisis was caused by banks lending too much money to unqualified borrowers and then holding overvalued real estate as collateral. Many buyers couldn't pay and the security wasn't there to cover the outstanding mortgage. And, it all came tumbling down.

When young entrepreneurs are just starting out, they probably don't have any significant net worth and their credit rating won't meet the bank's criteria for a business loan. Therefore, many young entrepreneurs are undercapitalized and our overall economic growth is held back. The keys to self-financing, which we'll discuss in detail later on, are to maximize profits and reinvest them into the business to fund the growth. Governments and banks could definitely do more to support start-up businesses, but, no pun intended, that's not an eventuality to bank on.

Another key growth factor is attracting labor. Many businesses that have strong positions in the market compete more for talented people than they do for customers. If your business has more orders than it can fulfill quickly, or more good ideas than you can productize in the near future, you may have this problem. As business cycles proceed on their roller coaster, which they are riding in the energy industry at the time of this writing, good companies are aggressively retaining their most valuable employees so that the companies can increase operations once the cycle swings up again. One of the most effective tools to reduce the labor pressure or constraint, especially for production people, is through the utilization of technology.

Technology is predicted to continue to decrease employment in manufacturing and other sectors within the next decade. Erik Brynjolfsson, a professor at the MIT Sloan School of Management, and his collaborator and coauthor Andrew McAfee state in their 2011 book, *Race Against The Machine*, that technology is having two important impacts on society. First, technology is dramatically increasing productivity and GDP (ergo, our comments on large corporations in productivity earlier in this section). Second, technology is destroying jobs faster than it is creating them, especially in manufacturing and positions where robotics and software can replace people. According to the authors' research, the United States and

China, the world's largest manufacturing engines, employ less people now than in 1997 *but produce significantly more output.*

This represents a huge opportunity for business owners to dramatically increase their productivity while reducing the negative impacts of a shortage of talented workers. Technology is also impacting professional roles in finance, law, and management that use data to perform analysis and make decisions.

Governments impact the business environment directly through taxation and indirectly with the time and cost of processing tax reports. The most progressive governments have tiered tax rates that are lower for smaller businesses and increase gradually as profits increase. Special tax credits for increasing payrolls and investing in technology are also useful to spur business growth. However, I always advise business owners to make investment decisions that will maximize long-term cash flow and not just minimize short-term taxes. *Many accountants have held back their clients' growth unintentionally by focusing on tax minimization, as per their training.* They should advise on maximizing long-term after-tax cash flow that creates wealth for owners.

In the United States especially, health care costs for employers have grown exponentially. According to the National Federation of Independent Businesses:

Since 2004, the average annual family premium for covered employees in small firms increased 69 percent. Family coverage insurance premiums for small firms increased from $9,950 in 2003 to $16,834 in 2014.

The average annual premiums for single coverage increased from $3,695 in 2003 to $6,025 in 2014.

Small businesses, on average, pay about 18 percent more for health insurance than their larger counterparts for the same group of services.

The cost of health insurance increased for 64 percent of offering small businesses last year, costs decreased for 6 percent.

Sixty-six percent of small businesses that experienced higher health insurance costs defrayed those costs through lower profits and 48 percent became more efficient/productive.

Some questions to consider:

- What technology can you access to overcome potential talent shortages?

- What appeal can you make to a bank that solidifies you as a proper credit risk?
- Are you doing things currently to raise and protect your credit score (e.g., retiring all short-term debt)?
- Are you focusing on maximizing long-term cash flow and not simply minimization of short-term tax liabilities?

You're Hired: Creating More New Jobs as Big Companies Downsize and Atrophy

Isn't it ironic that your biggest contribution to the economy is the biggest threat to your company?

Your biggest contribution is hiring more people. Privately held businesses are now creating 7 out of every 10 new jobs in North America.

Despite a hot economy in many sectors, big companies are cutting back. At this writing, energy companies are laying off employees as the price of oil hovers around its lowest price in a decade (and such cyclical trends will continue in many sectors). Governments are scaling back budgets due to decreasing royalty revenues in energy-producing areas. Target Stores just shuttered its entire Canadian operations and is putting 17,000 people out of work.

And, of course, technology will continue to erode need for human presence in many positions. Try reaching American Airlines on the phone and chatting with a human being. You'll be directed to the web, and if you refuse, you'll then confront a menu, then make menu choices, then be placed on hold, then hear announcements and ads, then be told that you can be called back within X minutes, and you'll accept these options still never having spoken to an American employee and the callback will late.

Your people are the biggest threat to your company because many don't see working in closely held businesses as a viable long-term career path, and your ability to wisely attract, evaluate, recruit, and nurture is probably not your world-class skill.

Many small and midsize businesses have positive cultures that are based on the founder's values, sincerely care about their customers, are active in the community, support local charities, and provide workplace flexibility for their employees. They have stronger relationships with customers and suppliers than larger competitors. Their service levels are more proactive and intimate than big box stores. Even though many private businesses offer these family and customer-friendly work environments, star employees may well not stay due to several factors.

> **Wealth Building Blocks:** Become personally involved in every new hire's onboarding and orientation, and obtain a coach to help you master these very crucial skills and behaviors.

Star employees can make more money working for a larger company (if they can get hired, and top talent almost always gets hired). Business founders are often technical people who worked on the tools first and became owners and managers second. Their management style is often focused on getting things done instead of taking a long-term and strategic view of growth. They're working *in* the business instead of *on* the business. Growth actually happens organically by increasing capacity to respond to customer requests. There is usually a lack of accountability due to the family environment. Family members may be in line for most promotions and this environment of nepotism will cause all but the weakest employees to leave.

Other challenges for small and medium enterprises include the lack of a formal organizational chart, lack of structured management reporting, multiple owners giving multiple and, sometimes, conflicting directives, and a lack of performance metrics that make it difficult or impossible to hold people accountable for results.

Despite these (fixable) weaknesses, small and medium enterprises are growing because of their unique value in the economy. They support and supply most of the Fortune 1000 companies with products and services. They are highly responsive to their customers' needs. Their personalized services allow larger companies to outsource noncore activities, which we'll discuss in detail in the next section.

Privately held businesses can continue their economic dominance and growth as employers by doing three things (Figure 2.2).

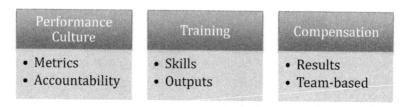

Performance Culture	Training	Compensation
• Metrics • Accountability	• Skills • Outputs	• Results • Team-based

Figure 2.2 Attracting and retaining talent

First, they must strengthen their cultures by focusing on performance. They can do this while they retain their friendly environments, provided that they are friendly with the best performers and tough on the nonperformers. The best place for your weakest employees and poorest customers is with your competitors. To hold people accountable, you need to set goals and measure performance against those goals. This is not done best in an annual performance review. This is done best by measuring daily productivity, such as actual production, and weekly results, such as sales or orders shipped on time.

Tip on Performance Metrics

Simply set up three categories and document performance against them:
- Exceeded expectations
- Met expectations
- Failed to meet expectations

Most companies should have almost all people "meeting expectations" unless they're having record year. If the company is not meeting expectations, but you rate most employees as meeting or exceeding, then you don't have a company, you have an employment agency.

Next, companies must position all of their employees for success by training them to develop their skills. Some owners resist training employees for fear that they'll leave and their investment will be wasted. That's the wrong perspective. The worst situation is actually an untrained employee who stays forever but never improves in productivity. The skills need to be focused on improving productivity, speed, quality, and value for customers. Employees also need soft skills in communication, listening, coaching, mentoring, supervising, and encouraging others to perform their best.

Finally, one of the easiest things to change but most difficult things to get right is compensation. An employee's compensation includes financial components such as salary, vacation, benefits, and bonuses. Nonfinancial components of compensation are very important because they can strengthen your culture, may not cost very much at all, and are valued highly by the employee. These include technology, tools, workspace, working remotely, flexibility of hours, and training investments.

Tips on Compensation

The research is very conclusive that employees are most motivated by gratification of the work and recognition for their contributions, *not* by money. If you give more money to an unhappy employee you'll create a *wealthier* unhappy employee.

Financial compensation can include a base salary and a performance bonus component of at least 10 percent of base and preferably 20 to 30 percent if you include sales people. The performance bonus should be based on two factors: the individual's performance and overall company results. We'll discuss this in greater length in Chapter 5.

By creating a culture that combines a corporate focus on performance with the family-friendly culture of the founders and their values, companies can attract and retain talent. Star employees want to know what their future opportunities are in the company. They want to know that they can grow with the company. And, they want to know that they'll be rewarded for their contributions to that growth.

Those can all be created and will generate a fantastic return on investment.

Supporting the Fortune 1000: Creating Unlimited Growth Potential for SMEs

Whom do global companies call upon when they need local repairs done on their multimillion dollar facilities? The Fortune 1000 companies are aggressively trying to grow their market share and boost their

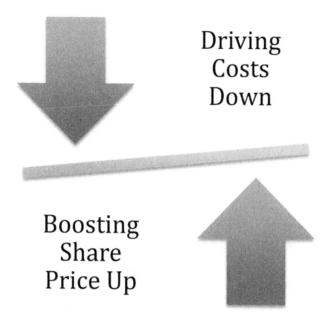

**Driving
Costs
Down**

**Boosting
Share
Price Up**

Figure 2.3 The outsourcing drivers

share price (Figure 2.3). They've determined to focus on their core strategies and customers and not be bothered with developing the expertise to repair their complicated equipment. The answer: They outsource repair and maintenance services.

Case Study:

EMW Industrial: EMW, founded by Ewen Morrison as a welding and repair shop (the EMW stands for Ewen Morrison Welding), responded to their international agribusiness and mining clients' need for expertise in managing their huge capital investments in conveyance and production equipment and ongoing expansion needs. EMW increased their capacity and expertise beyond solely reactive repair, to proactive maintenance and asset health management, beyond what these companies could do themselves. Then, they added construction services because their customers asked them for more help. As a result, *EMW grew annual revenues over 400 percent, and over 75 percent in one year*, as it built its reputation and capacity for "Safely Providing Quality Services," its corporate mission.

The Fortune 1000 companies are in an intensely competitive environment and are attempting to decrease costs while they simultaneously increase capacity and innovation. That's a tough combination: to get bigger and better while they try to get leaner and more profitable. Their answer is to move everything that is not directly valuable to their customers out from under their own roofs and plants. These huge companies want to minimize their investments in back office activities that don't add value to their customers or add profits to their companies.

This outsourcing philosophy creates huge opportunities for local and regional companies. In fact, even if you are a local company, you can quickly grow to become a major regional player as EMW did, by focusing on safety and quality work, and then scaling up capacity.[2]

Case Study:

Alaska Communications reduced labor costs by 66 percent and gained much needed flexibility to manage the highly variable load during the construction season. Using an approach developed by the company's supply chain manager, Kevin Kuper, who worked closely with supply chain consultant Rick Pay of the R. Pay Company in Portland, outsourcing with two key suppliers resulted in improved service levels, reduced costs, and enhanced capacity. In fact, the contractors used the same union as the company, so no union jobs were lost and no layoffs occurred. The suppliers provided personnel as needed to receive and dispense materials at the warehouses and submit restocking orders to the central warehouse in Anchorage.

The suppliers reaped several benefits from the new arrangement, including better communications with their customer (ACS), early notification of new project opportunities, and flexible hours for the warehouse location that better met their needs. The partnership between ACS and its suppliers had its rough spots initially, but trust, relationship, and strong communication helped all companies increase their capacity and profitability beyond what they could have achieved separately.

---

[2]Currently, and for several years, the trend has been to move "outsourcing" back to North America from overseas, cheap labor. Reducing consumer complaints and greater reliability have fueled this "onshoring."

Wealth Building Blocks: Anticipate your customers' needs and have solutions ready before you're asked to speed business and beat the competition.

Outsourcing is a reality because Fortune 1000 companies need to increase production while decreasing costs. Why can't you fill this need? The key opportunity for small and medium enterprises is to think much bigger. It's not about growing your business at 10 percent per year. It's about how quickly you can grow your business 1,000 percent, or 10 times as large.

Outsourcing works both ways. It is also an opportunity for small and medium companies to dramatically increase their production capacity, for example, by partnering with a larger company.

Case Study:

Castleton Industries manufactures grain, gravel, and flatbed logging trailers from high-tech steel that is actually lighter than some aluminum competitors, lasts much longer, and has a lower overall cost of ownership. Castleton was in growth mode and outsourced the manufacturing of a key assembly to a larger international firm that had sophisticated manufacturing and information systems. As a result, Castleton was able to double its production speed (and revenues) without any capital investment.

Key Questions: Who are the major companies in your area that require your services to expand their operations in a way that benefits from your knowledge of the local economy and customs? Conversely, which large companies can take on some of your production or service requirements and would enable you to significantly increase your output without any significant capital expenditures? How can you grow your business by 1,000 percent?

Let's turn now to how you can perpetuate the "thinking big" mentality through changes in ownership and control.

Trillions at Stake: The Upcoming Succession Crisis and What to do About It

How is your business going to provide for your financial future? Is your business like a gold mine that runs on autopilot and deposits bullion into your account every month or are you shoveling coal into the wheelbarrow and burning it for heat? Who will own your gold mine or coal mine in the future? Or will it become barren?

CIBC estimates the value of privately held business assets in transition will have a global impact of $1.9 trillion by 2017 and grow to $3.7 trillion by 2022.[3] A significant portion of this wealth—your wealth—is at risk because "close to 60 percent of business owners aged 55 to 64 have yet to start discussing their exit plans with their family or business partners."[4]

The correct time to begin planning an exit strategy is when the business is created. Quite a few of you are lagging behind that!

When done well, succession planning can transfer family wealth to future generations who can continue to grow the business, employ people, contribute to their communities and charities, and provide future opportunities for family members. When done poorly—or not done at all—a lack of succession planning can quickly destroy wealth created inside a business over decades, cause premature devaluation, result in job losses, increase family strife and hardship, and reduce the economic strength of communities and countries.

<u>**Case Study:**</u>
One business founder was fortunate to have a daughter who loved the business and worked in it from childhood. Although the daughter was the general manager and essentially running the business, the founder kept hanging on. The daughter got tired of waiting, left and started her own company. Key lessons: Founders need to let go. Successors need to step up. Talk about it before someone does something (or keeps doing something) that causes unnecessary family strife. Warning: Get your ego out of the way.

Some years ago, the Pritzker family, which founded and ran the Hyatt Regency Hotel empire, became embroiled in a bitter struggle over control, inheritance, and succession. The result was this family-owned monolith squandered billions—that's correct, billions—on lost valuation, legal fees,

[3]Tal, B. CIBC World Markets Inc. Inadequate Business Succession Planning—A Growing Macroeconomic Risk. *In Focus*, November 13, 2012. Retrieved March 2015 (research.cibcwm.com/economic_public/download/if-20121113.pdf).
[4]Ibid.

loss of productivity, and dismemberment. If it can happened to them, it can happen to anyone, and most everyone else isn't battling over billions but over a comfortable, debt-free retirement.

> **Wealth Building Blocks:** Never assume that the succession plan is obvious, that everyone is onboard, or that everyone will accede to your wishes. You'll require transparent plans and legal assistance.

My experience shows that succession planning starts in one of four places: the kitchen table, the boardroom, the hospital emergency room, or the funeral home (Figure 2.4). Two of these are not good. If you have started your succession, congratulations! Succession planning takes years. However, too many business owners avoid succession planning and put their business wealth and family security at risk. What are you waiting for?

> **Case Study:**
> MuniSoft. You met Donna earlier. She had to step out of semiretirement and go back into the business as the full-time president after her husband, the founder, passed away unexpectedly. Donna's son contacted me shortly after his father passed away and asked if I could help her regain control of her own company. I helped her build up her management team, promote an employee to become the new general manager, identify strategic opportunities for growth, and empower her team to grow the business. Over lunch recently, she shared that her company continues to grow, generating record revenues and record profits. Donna's management succession supported her business growth and wealth creation.

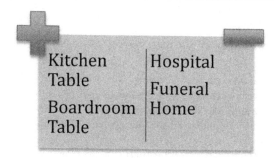

Figure 2.4 Where to start succession planning

According to a global survey by PriceWaterhouseCoopers,[5] 41 percent of respondents planned to pass ownership to the next generation. *But, more than half were not confident of their successor's skills.* Another 34 percent of respondents did not have a clear succession plan for their business upon their retirement. Therefore, approximately half don't have a clear plan or confidence in their successors. Twenty-five percent planned to retain family ownership and bring in nonfamily professional managers. Professionalizing management is an excellent step for a family to retain ownership while achieving growth under any ownership arrangement (Figure 2.5).

In the United States, 40.3 percent of family business owners are expected to retire by 2017 (if they can execute a succession plan), yet "less than half of those expecting to retire in five years have selected a successor," according to Conway Center for Family Business in quoting a Mass Mutual American Family Business Survey.[6]

In Canada, 50 percent of all business owners plan to exit their businesses by 2022, according to CIBC,[7] yet many do not have a clear succession plan or a successor identified.

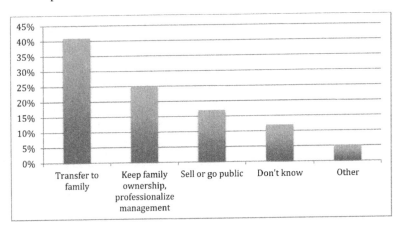

Figure 2.5 PwC Family Business Survey 2012

[5]PwC Family Business Survey 2012. Family firm: A Resilient Model for the 21st Century. Retrieved March 2015 (www.pwc.com/fambizsurvey).
[6]Conway Center for Family Business. Family Business Facts, Figures and Fun. Retrieved March 2015 (http://www.familybusinesscenter.com/resources/family-business-facts/).
[7]Tal, B. CIBC World Markets Inc. Inadequate Business Succession Planning—A Growing Macroeconomic Risk. *In Focus*, November 13, 2012. Retrieved March 2015 (research.cibcwm.com/economic_public/download/if-20121113.pdf).

Clearly, many business owners are not prepared for succession. They are placing their business wealth and financial security at risk. Are you?

Succession planning is really about two things: management and ownership. Dealing with them separately in a process I call "The Succession Two-Step" will make your decisions and planning easier. I'll explore succession planning in more detail in a later chapter.

Next, I'll discuss how small and medium enterprises can learn from each other. That's right, even your competitors can teach you something.

(For further information on these dynamics, there are free resources here: http://www.symcoandco.com/resources/)

Divided and Disorganized: Why and How SMEs Must Learn From Each Other

Do you have a competitor who pushes you to be your best? Would you like to learn more efficiently than through trial and error? What best practices can you learn from other successful companies?

Business success is based on continual learning and the application of that learning to generate results. Yet many business owners hold their best ideas close to the vest for fear that others will copy them. This secrecy, especially with the volume of free information available on the web, is unnecessary and ineffective. Taking ideas from other business owners, companies, and even industries, can help you to innovate and improve performance. Who are the most successful people that you can learn from?

The most effective learning environment for business owners is a small group of trusted peers who aren't in direct competition with each other. That's why business groups like Vistage, TEC (The Executive Committee), YPO (Young Presidents' Organization), Canadian Association of Family Enterprise's Personal Advisory Groups, and self-formed mastermind groups are highly popular and effective.

Alan facilitates global Growth Circles where consultants from around the world self-select peer groups that advise each other on business and personal development. Phil holds regular business lunch meetings where business owners are invited to attend and share their experiences and successes.

Trade associations are struggling to provide value to their members as the old model of an annual convention and regular newsletters don't provide advice when needed. Even though many are competitors in local areas, sharing of best practices can help all members to improve their businesses. Trade associations could improve their value by, for example, creating advisory groups or mentoring that matches senior, experienced people with newer members.

> **Wealth Building Blocks:** Competition opens markets, it doesn't narrow markets. Franchise owners of, say, Wendy's, build stores across the street from the MacDonald's franchise because they know people are accustomed to coming there to buy burgers.

Jeffrey Scott, a landscape consultant in Connecticut, holds "Leaders Edge" peer group meetings for landscaping business owners where they advise each other on best practices and share success stories. Jeffrey tests his ideas with the groups and then applies them in his major consulting projects.

Rob Nixon created coaching clubs for accountants in Australia where they openly share financial information (which they like to do because they're accountants) and advise each other on business growth. Rob holds participants publicly accountable for results. Business owners all need some level of accountability to raise their performance.

Alan, Jeff, Rob, and others also create constantly active "R&D labs" as their communities discover and recommend needs that their consultants and coaches should address.

The hierarchy of learning

There is a hierarchy of learning that applies to everyone (Figure 2.6). If you really want to learn something well, teach it to others. Initially, we learn through formal learning and personal experience. Ideally, we can learn interactively by helping others and having them help us. We can then share our knowledge and continually strengthen our learning by mentoring and teaching others.

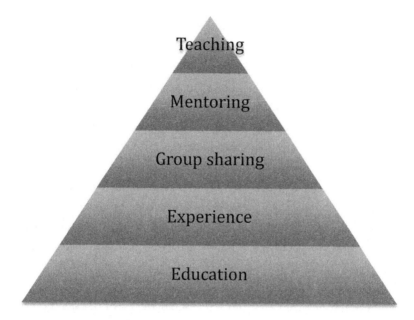

Figure 2.6 The learning pyramid

Now, let's apply the learning pyramid to your business. It's a family business best practice to require younger family members to obtain a formal education that can include both technical skills and business skills. What requirements do you have for formal education in your business?

Leading edge family businesses require their children to obtain a university degree or formal education. They also require them to work in other companies and obtain *two* promotions before they will be considered for employment in the family business. They run their company like a corporation with proper human resource management policies. This reduces entitlement, enhances family dynamics, and improves company performance. What experiences—and results—do you require your employees to obtain in order to be promoted?

Group sharing involves a small group that adheres to strict confidentiality. This environment of trust promotes the sharing of important information. We learn the most when we get our egos out of the way, become vulnerable, and ask for help on the important issues in our business and our lives. How can you set up a small group of trusted peers that can advise each other on business and personal issues?

Mentoring is an extremely powerful and beneficial process for both the person being mentored and the mentor themselves. Alan and Phil both mentor other business owners around the world and continually learn about new trends while observing common patterns among people. How can you utilize mentoring in your company?

Mentoring is a reactive methodology in which a trusted advisor is available with objective advice for the mentee.

Teaching at an industry event or a local college (or internally to work groups) can improve your personal presentation skills while forcing you to articulate your expertise. Many people have natural talents but find it difficult to explain those talents to others. Teaching, combined with writing, helps you to articulate your thought processes (perhaps your unconscious competence) so that others can apply them and help you grow your business.

Learning is a continual process; not a static event. That's the best part of building your team's skills: they continue to get more valuable and productive. That will make your job as a leader much easier as you strive to grow your business.

PART 2

Control and Confidence

CHAPTER 3

Leadership: You Can't Lead from the Engine Room

It's All About You: How Your Values, Vision, and Power Will Create Your Company's Future

When I was eight years old playing organized baseball, I got up to bat and my coach said, "Back up, boys, this kid can hit!" I didn't know I could hit until he said that, and then I swung for the fences. My coach, Bart Dowler, built up my confidence. That's what coaches and leaders do.

Who has taught you the most about business and life? Was this person a family member or highly driven entrepreneur? What attracted you to follow and learn from them? Who was telling others, "This woman is great!" or "This guy is the best!"?

The most critical factor in any organization's success, from a family unit to a service organization like the Girl Scouts, or a Fortune 500 company, is leadership. An effective leader has three key attributes that drive success: *a powerful vision, positive values, and the power to get things done.* You need power. You need to swing for the fences.

Henry Ford had a vision to create an automobile that everyone could afford. Bill Gates wanted a computer in every household. Steve Jobs wanted to make a disruption in lifestyles and provide people with beautiful, functional technology (and not the Dick Tracy "wrist radio"). While these world-changing entrepreneurs had huge visions, the simplicity of their vision was very powerful and we are all now far better off.

What is your vision for your company?

Take this vision exercise:

- How will your company look, behave, and create in the future?
- Where will you operate?
- How will customers benefit from your products and services?

- What dramatic and quantifiable values will you create for your customers?

Values are about what matters most to us and create the behaviors and ethical guidelines we willingly follow. Growing up playing street hockey and organized sports, I learned about fair play, good sportsmanship, losing gracefully, and shaking hands after every game.

The corporate values of a small or medium company always represent the owner's or founder's personal values, and that's a great competitive advantage. Your values give your company personality and character, and make you different.

Audio Warehouse, a regional home electronics retailer owned by Brian Melby and Don Rae, is celebrating 50 years in business. They compete successfully against the big box stores that spend millions on advertising by providing great service and advice. Their salespeople are professionals who build long-term relationships with their customers, and Audio Warehouse is thinking about the lifetime value of a customer, increasing repeat business, and generating referrals.

Visions, on the other hand, is a national electronics chain. When I purchased a navigation system for my daughter's car, the price included installation. On the day I went to book the installation, Visions required another 50 dollars to complete the installation or they wouldn't do the work! The manager was not in the store and we needed the work done. I paid the 50 bucks, walked out, and drove down the street to Audio Warehouse where I bought a new 55-inch television so the kids could watch movies downstairs (instead of hogging our TV). Visions doesn't have a very good vision of how to retain its customers.

The most powerful words that any military general, fire captain, or leader have ever said are, "Follow me!" Power comes from influencing others to perform their best in order to achieve goals that they're excited about and in ways that fit their personal values. (In most cases, the senior fire officer on the scene is expected to lead others into the fire scene.) A leader can only serve the needs of the stakeholders (family members, shareholders, customers, or employees) by generating results. That doesn't require the faddish "servant leadership." That requires powerful, results leadership. What kind of leader are you?

Leadership Quadrants

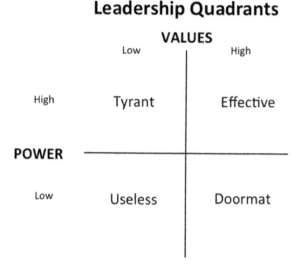

Figure 3.1 Leadership Quadrants

Figure 3.1 shows four possible leadership levels and all will have significantly different impacts on your organization. On the lower left quadrant, if leaders have poor values and low power, they're useless. Yet, in some organizations, such a leader may remain the leader because he or she owns all of the shares. This will not be a high-performing or valuable company.

A leader with poor values but high power and the ability to influence others will be seen as a tyrant. In poor economic times, people may be so desperate for a job that they'll put up with this environment until they can find a better employer. This situation is sustainable only when people (employees and customers) don't have a better option. The tyrant may even think that this personal style causes success. It doesn't; it's the barrier to greater success.

> **Wealth Building Blocks:** Leaders require strong values and power to create results.

A common leadership type is represented by someone who has good values but doesn't have the respect of others or the ability to influence them. This is common in family businesses where people related to the owner may have positional power due to their familial relationship, but they aren't respected because they don't, or can't, get things done on their own since they haven't learned to lead. *That's why it's important for family members to obtain formal educations and work at other companies before joining the family firm.*

The most effective leader is someone with strong values who attracts others with similar values and then has the power and influence to increase their confidence in pursuit of organizational goals. This applies to kids playing baseball and adults working at your company. What can you do to make working for your company as much fun as playing baseball? A lot depends on where you're standing.

You Can't Steer the Ship if You're Changing the Oil: How to Fire Yourself and Build an Effective Management Team

If you have to be at your business all of the time, you don't have a business; you have a job. There's only one way to fix that problem: You need to fire yourself out of day-to-day management and build a management team.

The four factors in accelerating growth and building business wealth are:

1. an effective management team
2. a clear strategy (which will be discussed in the next chapter)
3. real-time information on sales, production, and cash, and
4. working capital to fuel growth.

First, let's define a manager: someone who can hire people, fire people, spend money, and be held accountable for results. If a manager has to ask the owner to do any of these things on a regular basis, he or she is not a manager, but rather an overpaid employee. Many founders struggle at this stage with letting go of key decisions. It's at this point, often in the 5 million to 20 million of annual revenues, that the owner must make a critical decision: Get bigger or smaller, but you can't stay in that adolescent phase and control all decisions.

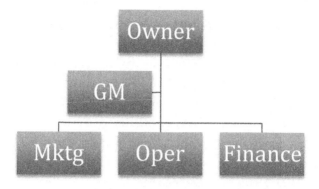

Figure 3.2 Small business management chart

For small businesses, typically under 10 million dollars in annual revenues, growth means that the owner needs to hire a general manager to run the day-to-day operations so the owner can transition to become the president. To complete the management team, the next hires need to be a marketing/sales manager, an operations manager, and a controller (Figure 3.2).

> **Wealth Building Blocks:** You must work *on* the business, not *in* the business.

As small companies grow to become mid-sized businesses, the management team and information systems must become more sophisticated. Ideally, you should (must!) hire people who have already been where you want to go. They've worked in larger companies that have formal processes, use budgets, respect monthly and quarterly reporting, and have information systems that provide critical business information in real time so that managers can make better decisions, faster. These people need to be held accountable—and compensated—for results. That's why planning is so important: resource allocation dictates strategic direction and speed (Figure 3.3).

Figure 3.3 How you spend your cash determines your strategy

Success in business requires a clear strategy, resources to support the strategy, and action in the marketplace to create results. Having a strategy without adequate resources or action will not generate results. Spending money and taking action without a clear strategy will not generate optimal results. Yet, it's amazing how many businesses are successful in spite of themselves just because of local market conditions (which, of course, are often unpredictable). A good management team will compare its results against plans and not be fooled by false positives.

A true team wins and loses together. This prevents the silo problems common in huge corporations where people lose sight of the fact that they're working for the customer to create value for the shareholders.

Here is an ideal management structure for a growing mid-market company (Figure 3.4). Note that the vice presidents on the left half of the chart (marketing and operations) are responsible for creating business results. The vice presidents on the right side (finance and HR) are responsible for providing resources (money, people) and measuring results. The president keeps everyone focused on short-term goals and aligned with the long-term direction. It's especially important in family businesses to bring in professional help that can guide and mentor family members for future leadership roles.

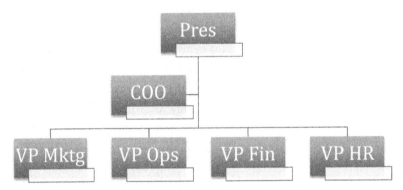

Figure 3.4 Midsize management organization chart

Case Study: Construction Company

A founder was growing his company very quickly. His bankers and major customers were very concerned about his lack of a succession plan. He brought in 10 employees into ownership. Some were family members but all worked in the business. These owners became leaders and managers and drove the company to revenue growth in excess of 300 percent. The shareholders elected a board of directors that meets quarterly. *They have made the shift from small business to mid-market company by strengthening the management team and implementing formal board governance.* The board oversees strategy, makes major financial decisions, and manages risks.

Business owners in high-growth companies must make the transition from owner to president as quickly as possible. Your role as president is to guide business operations in the proper strategic direction while maximizing value to your customers and increasing returns to your shareholders.

It is extremely important to think and act like a public company that pays dividends to its shareholders. That focuses management on generating positive cash flows to fund the dividends, and is an important part of building wealth, according to Kevin O'Leary, star of Shark Tank and chairman of O'Leary Funds. This is one of the key tenets of building business wealth: paying regular dividends. Even high-growth companies that need lots of cash to grow should be rewarding their investors (that's you) and building wealth for the owners along the way. Building wealth is a shift in mindset and culture from a singular focus on the customers.

The Chemistry of Culture: How Abundance Thinking Can Create Unlimited Success

The lens on my sunglasses popped out so I took my glasses back to Factory Optical, a fast growing retail chain, to tighten the frame. Kevin, my technician, said, "These lenses are cut too small for your frames. (I bought them at one of their other stores, much to Kevin's dismay.) I'll order you a new set of lenses. They'll be here next week." That's abundance thinking: taking care of the customer without minimizing short-term costs. It builds customer loyalty.

As a leader, you set the culture of your organization and impact— every day—your managers and employees, your customers, your suppliers, and your shareholders. Culture, the values and beliefs that guide behaviors, governs each of these interactions positively or negatively. Culture creates momentum and enhances relationships; everyone feels it and knows it.

The main weapon that privately held businesses have over much larger competitors, and why they can charge premiums for their products and services, is their culture. It's your focus on strong relationships, high responsiveness, customization, and speed that generate superior financial results (Figure 3.5). *Strengthening your culture is much cheaper than giving everyone a 10 percent raise where you would only end up with richer, not better, employees.*

Wealth Building Blocks: An unhappy employee will never create a happy customer. That's culture in a nutshell.

"You can't succeed without failing," said Michael Higgins, co-CEO of Mother Parkers Tea & Coffee, the fourth largest coffee roaster in North America. Mother Parkers acquired plants and installed leading edge equipment to continually improve their capacity and enhance their quality. They are playing to win.

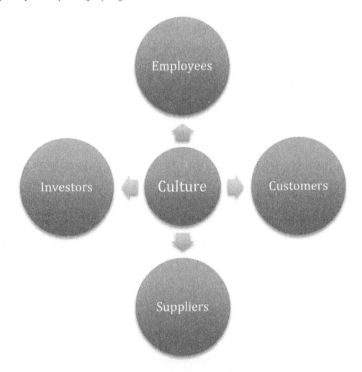

Figure 3.5 The chemistry of culture

Playing to win is about taking risks, launching new products and services, expanding into new markets, and trying new things in new ways. Yet, many privately held businesses see any failure as a risk that they can't afford to take. Or, even worse, the owner sees failure as a personal defeat because his or her ego is on the line with every decision. How do you view failure?

If your company is growing purely by organic customer demand, you are not growing fast enough. Your company will grow faster and more profitably if your culture is based on *proactively offering your customers ideas on how they can be more successful*. That's the essence of strategic growth. Doing so will strengthen your customer relationships, differentiate you from your competitors, and make you much more valuable. In other words, think and act like your own consultant and share ideas with your customer. Sharing is abundance thinking in action.

You are your suppliers' customer. Are your suppliers treating you as well as you treat your customers? Are you proactively communicating with your suppliers and openly sharing your important business information so that they can plan on how to serve you best? Or, are you continually putting price pressure on them and treating them like a commodity instead of a partner?

The best bankers with whom I deal aren't just suppliers of money; they're wise partners who can accelerate a business to greater success. Your bank has worked with larger companies than yours and can provide financial advice and resources to help you grow. That's worth an extra percentage of interest.

Investors want returns and those returns come from well-managed businesses that have strong strategic positions and generate positive cash flow. Abundance, to a shareholder, comes in the form of regular dividends. What is your dividend policy? How to you reward your investors?

Answer these key questions to assess your culture:

1. Customers: Do you have a philosophy that "the right customers are always right" and do everything you can to make them happy?
2. Empowered managers: Can they hire and fire people and spend money within their budgets?

3. Focus: How do you measure critical performance metrics such as "shipped on time" or "production" daily and communicate them to your team?
4. Accountability: How are employees and managers held accountable for performance, results, and customer satisfaction?
5. Positivity: How engaged are your employees in taking care of the customer?
6. Innovation: How often do employees share new ideas on how to do things better?
7. Leadership: How open are you to hearing new ideas from your people?
8. Confidence: Are your managers and employees playing to win; or playing not to lose?

Winston Churchill said, "Success is never final, failure seldom fatal; it's courage that counts."

Setting the culture can create effective momentum for organizational success. What about your success as a leader? We all know that it's lonely at the top.

It's Lonely at The Top: Utilizing Boards and Advisors to Achieve Your Potential

Every successful athlete, performer, and actor has an entourage of coaches and support staff to help them be their best on the field or on the stage. From nutrition and technical coaches to sports psychologists, these multimillion-dollar professionals don't go it alone. Who is helping you to be your best? (And all of them periodically change those coaches if the coaches don't help or if the performer outgrows them.)

When you first started your business, you may have held the worst job title in the world: owner/manager. That position doesn't come with an entourage. In fact, it's more likely to come with a very large nest of hungry birds—from employees to customers—that need to be fed and nurtured. You were the energy source for them. It needs to be the other way around.

When entrepreneurs first start out, they are dealing directly with employees, customers, suppliers, and bankers. That is not sustainable, nor optimal. The owner automatically becomes the general manager. As the business grows, they eventually hire a general manager, and the owner promotes himself or herself to president. This is the slow way to growth.

For fast growth, the key is to think and act like a president as soon as possible. That way, you'll get there more quickly. Here are the transition steps from owner to president (Figure 3.6).

Where are you?

A small business owner in the owner/manager role needs advice from his accountant, banker, lawyer, and insurance advisor. You can judge the value of your advisors by observing whether they offer proactive advice (most are lacking here) or just reactively respond to your questions. The latter is dangerous as you don't know what you don't know and they aren't helping.

A general manager who is not an owner needs support to manage a growing business. This normally comes internally from the president and externally from advisors.

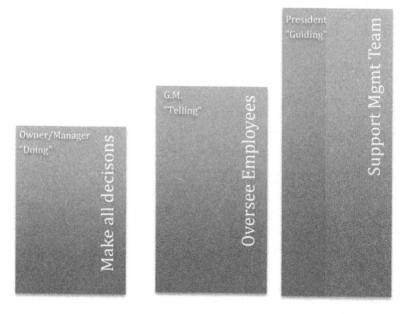

Figure 3.6 The leader's ladder

The president of a high-growth mid-market firm needs special help. Vern Harnish, the columnist on growth, writes that high-growth companies age quickly (like dog years), where a quarter or even a month can seem like a year in a larger, more stable organization, because of the dramatic changes taking place. Learning quickly is critical. Developing and implementing systems, often on the fly, is normal.

For high-growth leaders, advice from peers who have already traveled the path you're on is very valuable. In addition to a proactive team of professional advisors, peer groups such as Vistage, TEC (The Executive Committee), YPO (Young Presidents' Organization), and Canadian Association of Family Enterprise's Personal Advisory Groups are valuable. To be valuable, a peer group needs a strong leader who can facilitate and create both balance and momentum in the meetings.

A danger of these self-modulating peer groups is that your peers are limited to their own experience and perspectives. What worked for them may not work for you. In fact, it could be a path to disaster. Common sense and sound judgment are important.

Wealth Building Blocks: If you're the most successful person in your support group over a period of time, it's time to move to another support group where you won't be.

A viable option for small- and medium-sized enterprises is to create an advisory board of trusted peers. This is not a formal board of directors. An advisory board can include successful business people, perhaps a retired executive from a much larger business, and experts who are interested in helping you grow your company. They do not normally include your accountant or lawyer. They can include a good process consultant who is an expert in growth companies.

Take a moment: Who would be a great advisor for you:

1. _____
2. _____
3. _____
4. _____
5. _____

Speaking of consultants, there are two basic kinds. One is a content expert, such as marketing or human resources, who specializes in a functional area. The other, and preferred for high-growth companies, is a process consultant whose expertise is around what you are trying to achieve in terms of growth, building teams, increasing capacity, and going faster.

Regardless of business size, it's best to create the structure—and the mindset—so that you can run your business as a president. This can be a major shift for entrepreneurs who love what they do, grew up on the tools, and have become reluctant or accidental leaders because of their ownership position. The good news is that building a team of advisors and board members can help you to increase your success and maximize the growth potential and valuation of your company.

What got you here, as Marshall Goldsmith says, won't get you there. It's time to step out of your steel toe boots.

Now, let's look at your options for support (Figure 3.7).

As owners climb the leader's ladder, I'm frequently asked, "what does a president do?" As the president, you're responsible for, and need support on:

- setting the strategic direction of the firm to grow and become more valuable

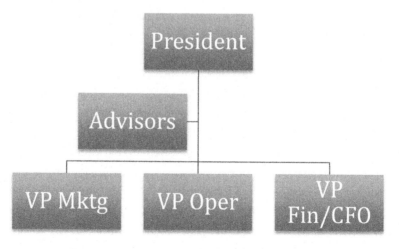

Figure 3.7 Supporting leadership

- implementing a succession plan for key managerial talent (not ownership, that's separate)
- developing a risk management plan that protects enterprise value
- guiding the entire organization into the future.

Larger businesses often have or are required to have a formal board of directors. Board members have a fiduciary duty to act in the best interest of the company, not just its leader. They may be responsible for government tax remittances such as payroll and certain taxes. This position comes with very specific responsibilities and requirements for formal meetings, sharing of information in advance of the meetings, and, most importantly, representing the shareholders. They aren't there to advise the president. *They are there to hold the president accountable.*

Next, we'll discuss how you can perpetuate your momentum by grooming your successor.

Leadership Succession: Why Management Succession is More Important than Ownership Succession

Who is your franchise player? That is, who is your star performer who will take the reins and continue to build your business wealth?

Tom Brady is the New England Patriot's franchise player. He has taken pay cuts to help the team stay within the salary cap. Most importantly, he has led the team to four Super Bowl victories. Mr. Brady willingly sacrificed a few million in salary to play for a winning team. *Are you willing to sacrifice some money (or equity) to retain a franchise player?*

There are three strategies for building your future leaders: franchise player, external professionals, and family successors (Figure 3.8).

One family business founder kept hanging onto the major decisions, even though his daughter was running the day-to-day operations. Eventually, the daughter got tired of not being listened to, and left to start her own company, which rapidly achieved dramatic growth, and is five times as large as her dad's company within a few short years. Had the founder listened and let his daughter lead, the company would have grown dramatically and the founder would have millions of dollars more of equity and wealth.

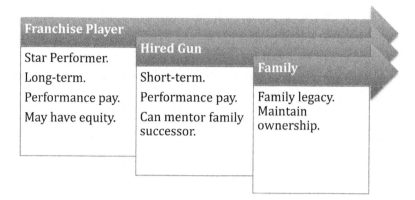

Figure 3.8 Leadership succession strategies

How is your wealth being impacted by your pride and ego?

Wealth Building Blocks: A lack of management succession triggers an ownership succession issue—it forces a sale—and it reduces the value of your company because you're selling a job, not a company.

Another business owner in the service sector realized that he was the primary rainmaker as well as the general manager. He brought in an experienced sales person, compensated him for performance, and introduced him to everyone he knew. He also moved the selling responsibility to the new sales person and away from technicians who generated revenues for their billable time but didn't bill for their sales time. Technicians are easy to find. Good sales people are not. *Your franchise player needs to take your business to at least triple the size.*

As your business grows, and it needs to grow just like a tree needs to grow, you need a bigger and better management team. A larger business generates more wealth, period. If your business is 5 or 10 times as large as it is today, and you don't have to be there to run the daily operations, then you've built a successful business. In fact, you've built your wealth, because now you have an investment that generates dividends and is building its (your) valuation. *Your wealth is your discretionary time!*

At the mid-market level, it's definitely time to bring in some fresh air by hiring professional managers. These should be in the major roles of marketing, sales, operations, finance, and even a new chief operating officer who oversees everyone else (as you become the real president, working on longer-term strategic issues). Many companies grew solely because of customer demand and have never marketed a day in their existence. Yet, the economy is global, and it's very easy to do business around the world. Marketing leadership will help you to expand into new markets and attract new customers. Hiring someone who has helped other companies to grow internationally, the hired gun approach, can accelerate your profits and growth.

Professional managers who have worked in larger companies bring great perspectives that high-growth companies need, from systems and reporting, to discipline and budgets. Many owners resist the perceived restriction of controls, yet it is these controls that allow the business to focus its growth and accelerate much more quickly. Controls are like the systems on a high-performance car: ensuring all components are working properly to enable high speed while maintaining safety and stability.

Family businesses need even more controls. They need family hiring and development policies to groom their own to be future leaders and owners. When Geoff Molson of the Molson brewing family graduated from college, he approached his father, the president of the Molson empire before it joined up with Coors, for a job.

"Son, we'll hire you when we see value in you," said the father. Shocked, Geoff went into the world where he built a successful reputation as a financial advisor and analyst. After gaining real-world experience, achieving promotions, and learning from other leaders, he was accepted into the family business. Today, Jeff Molson is the president of the Montreal Canadiens hockey club, which is partly owned by the Molson family.

Too many business owners don't groom their management team quickly enough, or at all, especially in family businesses. When the owner is ready to retire, there is no one in place to run the company, and that's a terrible mistake. The owner must sell the business and attempt to achieve ownership and management succession in one transaction. This costs the owner millions in lost equity due to lower valuation multiples from not having a professional management team in place.

Key Questions:

- What does your future management organizational chart look like, assuming that you will be at least five times as large?
- How are you grooming your future leaders?
- Which strategy, franchise player, hired gun, or family successor, will maximize your long-term wealth immediately?

Harry Rosen

Harry Rosen began selling men's clothing in 1954 and expanded to 16 stores and sales of almost $300 million. Last year, this iconic retailer was awarded New York's MR Magazine's award as one of the top 10 men's clothing retailers in the world. Harry's son, Larry Rosen, is now in charge, taking on international competition, and aiming for growth.

In an MR Magazine interview, Larry described the lessons that he learned: "My father has always been my inspiration…He established a culture and vision for this business: it's a passion for quality and high-end fashion…"[1] Larry has successfully carried on that culture.

Morsky Group of Companies

"In an SME, the challenge today is labor mobility," says Wayne Morsky, CEO of the Morsky Group. "Social media has created a platform where everything is shared, including employment. Getting to know and staying in touch with your labor force not only gives them a sense of belonging, but it also keeps your finger on the plus of what is happening day-to-day in an ever changing market," advises Morsky.

---

[1]http://www.mr-mag.com/harry-rosen-canadian-edge/ Accessed August 15, 2015.

CHAPTER 4

Strategy: It's all About the Results You Create

Meet the Morrisons

Why did you become a business owner?

Many business owners became entrepreneurs by accident: They had the family business thrust upon them, they were fired from the corporate world, or their hobby grew out of control until it consumed them and took over their working life!

Some of you may have been in the right place at the right time, like Ewen and Shirley Morrison. Cargill, the global food giant, asked Ewen, a farmer and welder, if he could make repairs on the top of their local grain elevator, 120 feet above the ground. Ewen replied with what all great, aspiring entrepreneurs say to a Fortune 100 company seeking to spend money: "Of course!"

Ewen and Shirley stayed up all night taping welding cables together so that Ewen could reach the top of the grain elevator from his welding truck, 12 stories below. Today, Ewen and Shirley, along with 15 other family and managers, own and operate EMW Industrial Ltd, a successful mid-market company with 200 employees serving the agriculture and mining industries across western Canada. Ewen's business grew dramatically and quickly because he aligned his passion for agriculture with his skills in welding, fixing machinery, and taking care of his customers. Shirley's eagle eye helped to keep billings up to date and the cash coming in. From humble and hardworking beginnings, came a mid-market company that makes a significant economic impact to its employees, customers, and suppliers.

A company can maximize its economic impact and business success by having a clear business strategy based upon conditions that it creates or merely arise. This chapter will give you a framework to accelerate your top-line revenues, your bottom-line profits, your cash flow, and your business wealth.

Some Definitions of Importance

First, let's define strategy: *It's the intentional focus and alignment of your resources to provide maximum value to your ideal customer with maximum return for you.*

Water, when it's focused at 60,000 pounds per square inch (psi) of pressure, can cut through two inches of steel. When it's not focused, water splashes around and causes rust, thus weakening the steel. Your ability to focus your value on your ideal customer and align your talents, time, people, money, expertise, and energy are critical to accelerating your profits and growth.

Here is our model for accelerating your business success (Figure 4.1). We call it the M5 Growth Accelerator (perhaps to be confused with BMW's high-performance M5 sedan!).

Figure 4.1 The M5 growth accelerator

First gear: Mindset

Mindset is about you, your personal drivers, and how to create a strong and sustainable business strategy around you and your talents.

There are some basic questions to consider (Figure 4.2):

1. What are the personal values and beliefs that guide your attitudes and actions?
2. What are your personal goals and objectives for owning, operating, managing, and growing your business?
3. What are your natural talents, passions, and personal strengths?
4. What is your optimal business strategy given your responses to the above?

Mindset is about your passion and connection with your business. It's the degree to which you can synergize your family and personal goals with your business and professional goals so that you have a clear and present focus in your life, without conflict.

Beliefs

Beliefs are the values that govern your behaviors, sometimes unconsciously (core beliefs, such as the value of honesty) and sometimes consciously (operating beliefs, such as listening carefully to customer complaints).

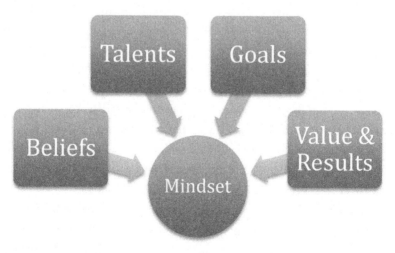

Figure 4.2 Mindset maximizer

Wealth Building Blocks: What you think and the words you use to think inform your behavior, which influences others.

We have over six decades of combined business and consulting experience. Years ago, Alan felt that most small businesses' number one problem was a lack of working capital. Phil believed that businesses didn't have cash flow problems; they had marketing problems. They now both agree that the number one problem facing entrepreneurs is self-esteem. *Self-esteem, or more specifically, a lack of self-esteem, causes both working capital and marketing problems, and reduces wealth potential.*

If business owners have low self-esteem, they will lack confidence in identifying and communicating their true value to the market. Therefore, they will likely undercharge for their product or service and fail to negotiate payment terms that favor their business. We see this occurring daily in small businesses around the world.

This is increasingly common when small companies sell to much larger companies. If the small business is desperate to get the sale, it will acquiesce to the larger company's downward price pressure or accept 60-day (or increasingly 120-day) payment terms. This causes working capital problems, especially for companies in high growth mode. (Remember, you are not your customer's bank. A small company should never carry a larger business for more than 30 days.) Despite having strong top-line sales and even good bottom-line profits, a company can quickly run out of cash. Growth will accelerate your burning up of cash. We'll talk more about this in the Monetization section below.

What are your personal values and beliefs? If you think that business is a highly competitive, dog-eat-dog, win/lose, zero-sum environment, then you'll be either in an aggressive or in a defensive position. You're fighting over a larger piece of a set pie. If you think that business is about synergy and helping your clients and customers to be more successful, then you'll be in a collaborative mode to help your customer and yourself to make the pie larger. The latter is a more positive and realistic mindset.

These values, consciously or subconsciously, drive your behavior and how you present to, and negotiate with, your customers. What personal values are accelerating or slowing down your business growth and wealth creation? How can you align your values with your goals and your talents to increase your focus and your results?

Talents

We all have natural talents. We all have these qualities in low, moderate, or high amounts: attention to detail, tolerance for repetition, comfort with ambiguity, persuasiveness, and assertiveness. (See, for example, *Social Style/Management Style* by Dr. Robert Bolton and Dorothy Grover Bolton.)

For any position in your company, use the line chart shown in Figure 4.3 to assess the ideal talents required for high performance.

For example, your accountant needs high attention to detail and high repetition, but not strong assertiveness. The accountant doesn't need much persuasiveness or assertiveness to create reports. Things get interesting, though, when the accountant is promoted over time to manager, vice president, and ultimately becomes the chief financial officer.

The CFO is not hands-on with computer input so needs less attention to detail and repetition. However, the CFO is now an important part of the senior leadership team and needs to advise on the financial impacts of planned strategies. He or she needs to communicate and persuade others and to assertively protect the value of their company while maximizing growth and returns for shareholders. There will be conflicts among competing interests that require strong persuasion and assertiveness to resolve.

Position: _____

	Low	Medium	High
Attention to detail			
Repetition			
Persuasiveness			
Assertiveness			

Figure 4.3 The talent assessment chart

You can see how the lines for these roles invert. That's why a good CFO is hard to find in the accounting department and why Phil retired from accounting after just two years. His profile is that of a CFO, financial strategist, and management consultant.

You can apply this exercise to all of your positions and employees. The patterns change for roles required as people are promoted from technical to management and then leadership roles, but people don't change. Now, apply the talent assessment process to your line functions: the key people in sales and operations.

Here are the steps. First, identify the ideal talents for your positions. Then, ask supervisors to assess your staff using this framework. The next step is to ask your employees to assess themselves. Finally, compare the results and see where you have good fits and where you are creating stress and friction by trying to square a circle. We've seen poor fits all the way from presidents to the shop floor.

(This talent framework can also be a useful career planning tool for your kids. Given the high cost of education these days, we're surprised that this tool isn't used as career selection for high school students and their parents.)

Wealth Building Blocks: Talent is the owner's off-balance-sheet main asset.

The talent assessment does not need to be done by the human resources department. We think the HR department is unnecessary in most organizations, anyways. Other than for payroll and benefits, the responsibility for performance management should be with the employee's direct supervisor. When you hold those supervisors responsible for performance and reward them for results, wonderful things can happen in your business.

As your roles have evolved, from operations to general manager to president, how have you utilized your talents differently? Where do you need to create systems or strengthen your management team to compensate for your weaknesses? Are you leveraging your strengths as much as possible? This reflection can add a lot of power to your position, reduce stress and drag, and increase your speed to success. (Create high psi, don't enable rust.)

Once you've identified everyone's natural talents, it will be much more effective to create personal goals that they can achieve and that are aligned with overall business goals and strategies.

Goals: Synergizing Personal and Professional Objectives

Your role as a business owner is simply to identify the ideal lifestyle that you want and then design your business to support your personal goals. You aren't fuel for your business; your business needs to be fuel for your personal life. Goals will synergize your personal and professional objectives so that you are consistently aligning resources and headed in the right direction.

The start-up phase might require lots of hours with little return, but that period needs to be as brief as possible. Sometimes we see small businesses with 10 years of existence struggling because they keep having the same year of experience over and over and never get out of the start-up phase. A small business requires a management team, an information system, and working capital to grow and become a mid-market company. It's that simple and straightforward.

On a recent business trip, Phil watched a reality television program where a mechanic bought old clunkers and fixed them up to be high-performance classic vehicles. The head mechanic had a philosophy that "every engine wants to run." We believe that every business wants to grow. The best way for your business to support your lifestyle is through growth.

How would you rate yourself in each of the following four main categories? Give yourself an "A" if you're doing very well, "B" for good, "C" for average, and "D" if it needs improvement.

1. Health, including physical, mental, emotional, and spiritual.
2. Relationships, including family, friends, social, and professional.
3. Financial, including earnings, cash savings, investments, retirement, education, insurance, and other protection.
4. Lifestyle, including where you live, how hard you work, vacations, and whatever else is important to you.

How did you do? Your business is likely making a multimillion-dollar economic impact in your community based on your contributions to your employees' payroll, your customers' results, and your suppliers' sales. *Yet, are you taking as good of care of yourself as a multimillion-dollar athlete does?* Do you get regular exercise, eat healthy food consistently, sleep well, and obtain valuable advice from coaches who specialize in everything from attitudes to yoga? You are your company's most valuable asset and the main creator of business wealth for your family.

The Value of Results: Don't Confuse Strategy with Planning

We defined strategy as the intentional focus and alignment of your re-sources to provide maximum value and results to your ideal customers and maximum return for you.

Here are a few examples of clear strategy from our clients:

- Knight Archer Insurance is about "Making Life Easier" for their personal and business clients by providing an integrated and convenient full-service brokerage that includes personal lines coverage, motor vehicle and fleet insurance, life and disability insurance, mortgage financing, business insurance, and special services for high net-worth individuals.
- MuniSoft develops and supports software and provides educational seminars to help administrators of rural municipalities to manage their tax rolls and serve their taxpayers. The company holds a strong number one market share position in its key markets and is an important source of expertise for its customers and governments.
- McKenna Distribution Ltd. is a high-growth company that is combining the distribution of flooring and renovation products with the custom manufacturing of counter tops to provide a robust offering for contractors, home builders, and home owners.
- Peter Crushing and Hauling helps construction companies and government entities to improve their asset utilization and infrastructure by planning multi-year product needs and managing product resources and inventories.

- The R. Pay Company provides consulting expertise to help its mid-market clients generate higher financial returns by improving operations and developing strong collaborations with suppliers and customers.
- The Grew Co. helps its clients to "Do Business Faster" by aligning strategy, metrics, and accountability to support growth initiatives in a variety of businesses and industries.

Wealth Building Blocks: Strategy is top-down and freeing, planning is bottom-up and restricting.

All of these companies are proactively focused on providing their specific value to their ideal customers. They don't overreact to every prospect's inquiry. They qualify prospects to ensure a good fit with their strategy and then deliver a consistent product or service. They focus on providing value to their ideal customer to increase that customer's results. That's strategy in action (Figure 4.4).

Planning, on the other hand, is about doing what you did last year and perhaps adding three percent to the volumes and dollars. It's incremental and begins where you left off last year. That's ridiculous and no

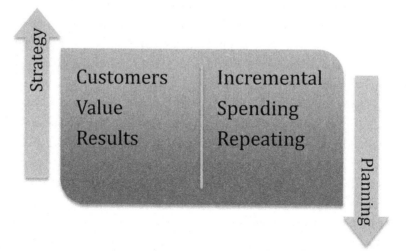

Figure 4.4 Strategy vs. planning

way to grow a company or increase your business wealth in a dynamic business environment. Although the mathematics of projections with a three or five percentage increase are easy to calculate and can give some people comfort that "we have a plan," there is no validity to whether your customers want more of the same and how much more.

Business is a contact sport and you need to become integrated into your customers' businesses as a strategic partner, not just a vendor, to help your customers be successful and to grow your business along the way. Strategy, simply put, is about increasing your customers' success. Your success will follow. Planning without strategy is the flawed thinking that what worked yesterday will work tomorrow.

> **Wealth Building Blocks:** Focus on the results that your products and services create for your customer. Don't focus on the inputs; analyze the outputs. That's where your optimal value lies. When you quantify your value, you can attract your ideal customer, and maximize your price, your profits, and your wealth.

Despite our frequent criticisms of airlines, both Southwest and WestJet (its Canadian copycat) are generating profits in an industry plagued by losses, bankruptcies, and questionable mergers. Both of these airlines focus on running one or two models of planes which simplifies everything from inventory to pilot training and repair times, thus reducing costs and decreasing repair times. How can you simplify your operations to reduce costs and increase speed and profits?

Here's an example of simplifying work processes (Figure 4.5). I worked with R.H. Electric, an electrical contractor who was experiencing strong growth due to an increase in the local economy, but was lacking control of the day-to-day business. To meet this new demand, the company needed to do things differently. They generated a 25% increase in operational capacity and top-line revenues from four key steps, and without any capital expenditure. They got control of all of their projects by making their schedule visible on the wall. Next, they identified which team members had the experience to deliver the project the fastest. They involved the project crew leader in all aspects of planning the project, determining materials and equipment needed, and thinking ahead of possible obstacles and delays. Finally, they started tracking their project time daily and recording it against the time budget so that they could react quickly if the time incurred was out of sync with the expected progress.

The result was a dramatic increase in buy-in from the crew leaders, more planning and organization up front resulting in fewer delays, and faster delivery to happier customers at better margins. The impact: they grew a three-million-dollar business into a four-million-dollar business quickly. The increase in EBITDA (earnings before interest, taxes, depreciation, and amortization) was $300,000 and the increase in company valuation . . . and the owner's wealth . . . was five times EBITDA or $1,500,000. That's the economic impact of working smarter, not harder.

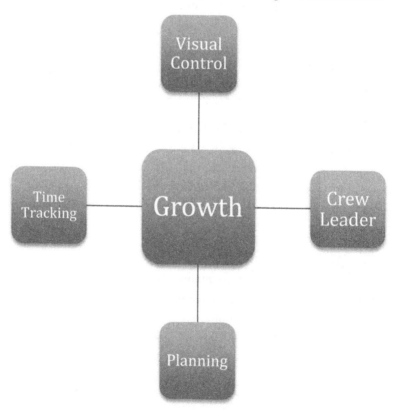

Figure 4.5 *Growth steps for contractors*

To grow your business to 5 or 10 times its current level, you can't work 5 or 10 times as hard as you're working now. But, you can increase your business profits and valuation dramatically through clarifying your strategy, strengthening your management team, providing the team with information that accelerates and enhances decision making, and improving your processes on how you deliver your products and services. Growth is about mindset. It's about thinking differently.

Phil was once a partner in a construction company that provided drywall installation to new homebuilders. His company didn't compete on price, because that would be a race to the bottom that no one could win. They focused on building relationships with the homebuilders' managers and showed how they could be trusted to deliver a high-quality product on time and on budget so that the managers could hit their targets and maximize their bonuses.

> **Wealth Building Blocks:** All marketing messages and negotiations should focus on the other person's self-interest.

The company guaranteed the quality of their work and did touch-ups after all the other trades people had finished their work and occasionally dinged up the smooth walls. The major competitive advantage was that they could attract and retain skilled talent in a highly competitive labor market and they had the supervisors to oversee production. The management advantages were:

- daily control of every project
- issuing an invoice in 10 minutes flat (some contractors are so busy that they don't have time to issue an invoice and that's a temporary condition that will be cured when the contractor runs out of cash and crashes the business)
- working capital to fund growth.

How quickly can you issue an invoice? How much growth can your working capital handle?

Companies with weak strategies are easier to find. The most common problem is a carryover from a company's cash starved start-up days where they tried to be all things to all people and do anything for a quick buck so they could meet payroll. This isn't a strategy. It's the absence of strategy. What are you still doing that's carried over from your start-up days that is diluting your brand, distracting your focus, and costing you more than you know?

Another weak strategy is when a company sits back and waits for the phone to ring and orders to roll in. How many of their competitors are out there developing new products and services, bragging about their customers' successes, and building relationships with prospects (including your customers)? What percentage of your sales is driven from reactive order-taking vs. proactive marketing and sales?

Our current example of a large company with a poor strategy is Sears Canada. Phil and his wife bought Sears appliances when they moved in to their home about six years ago. Wisely, they bought the extended warranty. Little did they know that the extended warranty included extended stress. Here is how Phil's wife, Kerry, explains it: *"It's been one year of attempting to get the vacuum fixed. It's been four months since our vacuum has worked properly. We've had numerous technicians who have visited us, diagnosed the problem, ordered the parts, received the wrong parts, showed up without parts, changed their minds, and then just stopped showing up at all."*

Sears Canada's US parent company recently reduced its equity investment in the Canadian subsidiary. The majority shareholder was injecting funds into the business. This is a major company on a downward slide to oblivion because they aren't taking care of the customers that they already have while they continue to spend millions in advertising trying to attract new customers.

Research in Motion, the Canadian company that brought the popular Blackberry to the world several years ago, did not focus on its core competence of corporate security for the wholesale market. Instead, they tried to compete with the device makers who were creating stylish and user-friendly smartphones for the retail market. Apple and Samsung are crushing Blackberry in the market because they design products that people like and that work very well. (And Apple is dominating Samsung because it has created rabid customer loyalty.) What do your customers want, and are willing to pay a premium for, that you could deliver quickly without significant capital expenditure or development costs? Your most powerful weapon for growing your business and building your wealth is your business strategy.

Strategic Driving Forces: How to Focus and Increase Your Value

Strategic drivers, based on the work of Ben Tregoe and John Zimmerman (*Top Management Strategy: What It Is and How It Works*), that are most relevant for closely held businesses are the areas that exert the greatest influence over the nature and direction of the firm, and include:

1. Products and services offered: A trailer manufacturer, construction company, or specialized service company such as a scale company typically does one or two things very well for its customers.
2. Markets served: A closely held business that provides multiple products and services to a specific market, such as a boutique accounting firm for privately held businesses, or an industrial service company that offers predictive maintenance for mining companies are examples of markets served driving force.
3. Technology: A computer service or software company is based on helping customers utilize technology to grow their businesses.
4. Method of distribution: McDonald's franchisees sell hamburgers and coffee. Tim Hortons sells donuts and coffee. Nobody goes to a McDonald's or a Tim Hortons to shop; they go to purchase. They will sell any related food items consistent with their distribution outlets. (Some people claim McDonald's is actually in the real estate business.)
5. Method of sale: A catalog company can sell any item, from toothbrushes to lawn mowers, with its careful lists and solicitation to those lists. Sporty's, Griot's Garage, Hammacher Schlemmer, and B&H Photo are some examples.
6. Natural resources: An oil and gas firm or a gravel-crushing company may own its own reserves, and a corporate farm utilizes farmland.
7. Production capability: This is less common for SMEs. However, professional service firms need to keep their professionals billable. This is where hourly billing can conflict with the client's goals of obtaining service and advice quickly and why we recommend value-based billing, which Alan pioneered for the consulting profession, for all professional firms. For more information, see Alan's book, *Value-Based Fees* (Jossey-Bass/Pfeiffer).

Wealth Building Blocks: You DO have a driving force, but you may not have consciously set it.

Your exercise is to determine your strategic driver. Once you know what your primary strategic driver is, it will be easier to set your strategic goals and direction. However, a major problem with strategy is that many consultants and executives run around conducting strategic planning sessions. That's an oxymoron in our book, because the planning is usually incremental and based on where you are now. You'll rarely hit your strategic goals. We recommend that you first set your desired future state, or what we call your *"strategic future"*, and then work backwards from your goal. That's the fastest and most effective way to dramatically build your business wealth.

Otherwise, planning kills strategy.

For example, I mentioned EMW Industrial at the beginning of this chapter. When I first started working with them, they were primarily a repair company that fixed things when they broke down. My strategy process clarified that EMW's value was in their expertise and knowledge not only in how to repair things, *but also to predict which things needed repair and in what order, and how to increase overall production capacity.* In other words, they became proactive advisors to their clients, who are global agribusiness and mining firms. The ability to advise their clients on how to allocate resources most effectively to help maximize up-time, extend asset life, increase capacity, and decrease costs was hugely valuable on an advisory capacity alone.

EMW acquired new skills and promoted this proactive value to their Fortune 500 clients. As their large customers were downsizing and seeing senior people retire, EMW's value became even more critical. This strategic focus increased revenues with existing customers and attracted new customers resulting in 377% revenue growth. EMW also implemented the major steps that any mid-market company needs to grow. They expanded their management team. They tracked project activities on a daily basis and shared information with project leaders and managers. They built strong relationships with bankers to fund the growth. And they always focused on Ewen's core values as demonstrated in their mission: Safely Providing Quality Services. EMW aligned their tactics with their overall strategic value.

Note from Figure 4.6 that excellent tactics are only one part of a success equation, and that a clear and present and communicated strategy is what creates the proper mindset.

The most important factor in your business growth and wealth building is your mindset, comprised of your beliefs, talents, goals, and values. This mindset will guide your business strategy. Once your strategy is focused, it is much easier to develop marketing, methodology, monetization, and metrics. Many companies skip the discipline of strategy only to spin their wheels in the other areas because they lack a clear direction. Phil uses this M5 model to help companies create their strategies in six hours. You may access a free copy of the Six Hour Strategy toolkit here http://www.symcoandco.com/resources/articles/sixhourstrategy.

Once our mindset is in the right place we can shift to the next gear: Marketing.

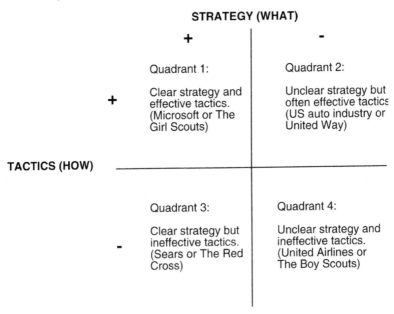

Figure 4.6 The strategy/tactics comparison

CHAPTER 5

Talent Scout: Turning all Employees into Recruiters and Producers

Performance Management: Always Begin with the End in Mind

Performance management is about managing the inputs—time, people, money, resources—to maximize the outputs. How do you continually increase your employees' performance? The idea is maximum outputs with minimal inputs, which is the basis for dramatic ROI.

Performance management is more than metrics; it's about results. Results come from your strategy, your leadership mindset, and your culture. It looks like Figure 5.1:

Figure 5.1 Performance management factors

Results include the outcomes that you generate for your customers and the minimization of resource expenditures, as well as the performance of your own company.

Answer these questions to assess your performance management.

1. How do your front-line employees describe your strategy?
2. How are your leaders held accountable for achieving your strategy?
3. In what ways does your culture reinforce your strategy?
4. What results are desired, supported, and rewarded in your company?

The key philosophy of this book, and the fastest way to build your business wealth, is to focus primarily on the results that you create for your clients and customers.

> **Wealth Building Blocks:** Measuring and communicating your customers' successes will enhance your performance faster than any quality or efficiency incentives, because your employees will be focused on helping someone else.

External results are based on your customers' performance, such as increasing their sales or profits or market share. Internal results are about you. The best-performing companies are aligned with providing as much value to their customers as quickly as possible, as we described in the preceding chapter on strategy.

EMW Industrial changed its strategy and focus *from repairing equipment to maximizing their customers' equipment uptime,* increasing production, and improving ROI on capital expenditures. When this strategy changed, EMW started measuring their customers' uptime and impact on production volumes. Now, EMW's employees are focused on their customers' results. That's how you create a culture of performance. You measure what's important.

The best construction companies don't just focus on completing projects on time and within budget. They help their customers to improve the project management process. They recommend ideas that reduce the long-term cost of ownership, make ongoing maintenance easier, and lower future costs.

The key to performance management is to measure an individual employee's contributions to customer results (externally) and to your business results (internally). Now, you may think that's difficult, but it isn't. It's the inverse of activity-based costing, a process developed by management accountants. Activity-based costing focuses on the time to complete a task and the related labor and overhead allocations attached to that time. Results-based costing, on the other hand, measures the results obtained per time and dollar.

To measure external results, ask your customer if they're happy. It's that easy. Ask them if they received the order or service when they needed it and in the way they wanted it. Ask them how they use your product or service in their business. Ask them what ideas they have to make the product or service easier to order, receive, store, and utilize. Now, you will have information that most competitors won't and that you can use to improve your strategic value.

You see, everything that you do in your business is ultimately about strategy. And, strategy is about improving your client's condition by providing maximum value as quickly as possible.

To measure internal results, focus on three key factors:

- Shipped-on-time (according to manufacturing expert Rick Pay)
- Production-per-employee
- Profit-per-employee

When you measure an employee's production and their profit, it will be extremely easy to rank your employees. Then, you can determine what the best ones do differently and better so that you can enhance the next best employees' performance to the highest levels. Don't waste time trying to elevate the worst performers to become like your best performers until you've determined the cause.

When dealing with poor performers, you need to determine the cause. It will be a lack of training/resources, a poor fit of skills/talents, or a poor attitude. If an employee has a good attitude and wants to learn something, then training will either work or it won't. If it doesn't work, then you're not utilizing their natural talents in the best way. A simple, non-HR department test for talents is to ask the employees what they like to do in their free time. This will indicate some of their natural talents.

Here's the acid test according to Robert Mager: Ask if they could per-
form if their life depended on it. If they can't, then you have a skill
problem. If they can, then you have an attitude problem.

The best place for employees (and customers) with poor attitudes is
with your competitors. Many business owners hire too quickly and fire
too slowly. If someone doesn't fit and doesn't want to perform better,
then let them go. You'll be doing everyone a favor.

Performance management is about positioning your employees for success and measuring the results. In fact, every employee should be providing
you with a minimum of 200 percent and preferably 300 percent or higher
return on investment in wages. What's your employee ROI?

I've seen some employees take calls at 4:58 pm and others refuse, because they want to bolt out the door at 5 pm. What kind of employees
do you have? Are they simply putting in a day or are they putting in
their talent?

Once you've created a performance culture, it will be much easier to
attract the right new talent to your company.

Recruiting is Like Shoe Shopping:
How to Ensure the Perfect Fit?

Do you know anyone who will wear a great pair of stylish shoes even
though they are very uncomfortable and will actually hurt their feet?
When it comes to recruiting, you need both style and fit. But if you
don't get the fit right, then the style won't matter. And if you pursue
only style, your feet (business) will hurt almost immediately.

Recruiting effectively is the key to increasing your long-term capacity, improving your management bench strength, and enhancing company valuation. In fact, high-growth companies focus as much or more on
adding talent as they do customers. If you don't have the talent to perform the work, then the customers won't be happy and will leave.

One organization spent five months hiring a young professional.
Their culture was to go slow and involve many levels in hiring decisions.
Eventually, they offered the professional a position. The professional,
who was entrepreneurial, lasted eight days, and quit. Neither the company nor the professional recognized their vast differences in their DNA.

I've seen companies hire reactively and too quickly to fill a vacant position. They take the first warm body that looks good enough. Then, when it's clear things aren't working out, they fire too slowly. Do you have any employees who are clearly a poor fit for your company but you are hoping will stretch and turn into an ideal employee? A good leather shoe will stretch a little bit but not that much (unless the leather is cheap). You don't try to "wear in" employees like shoes.

Wealth Building Blocks: Building on an employee's natural talents will improve performance faster than any combination of posters on the wall and company sing-a-longs.

Hiring for the right fit in the first place, instead of just style, will provide a much higher return on recruiting. Here are three ways to try on those new recruiting shoes and test them for fit (Figure 5.2).

If you hire someone who fits the culture and has talent, but can't collaborate well, you'll have a lone wolf.

If you hire someone who has talent and can collaborate but doesn't fit the culture, you have someone who will be rejected by the organizational immune system.

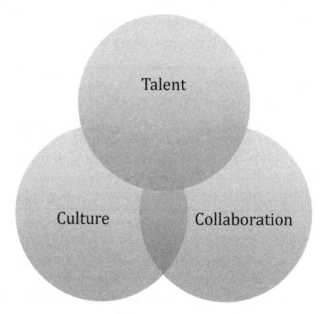

Figure 5.2 Recruiting criteria

And if you hire someone who fits the culture and can collaborate well but doesn't possess native talent, you have a non-starter, a poor performer.

How often have you heard an executive say, "We hire for attitude and train the technical." That's flawed. Unless the person has the core talents, the training will never work. We all have natural talents and skills that flourish in the right role. One key to hiring for fit is to assess and understand the prospective employee's natural abilities in terms of the key job requirements: learning, interacting with customers and employees, performing repetitive tasks, responding to ambiguity, being assertive, persuading others, and handling stress.

Does your human resources department recruit according to a 20-page job description? That's just crazy. What are the two or three most important results—outputs, not inputs—that this person is responsible to create? Focusing on results will help you to attract the right person. *Job descriptions are usually worthless because they focus on tasks, not results.*

The organizational culture, and how its values and beliefs influence behaviors, is the most important overall criteria for hiring, *after* you've established that a person has the talents to do the job. Your culture is your DNA for taking care of the customer, for continually improving your value and for strengthening your teams and individuals.

Case Study:

A midsized accounting firm tried to outsource its business development function to sales people who were paid for success. The conservative nature of the accounting industry and the importance of business clients getting to know their accountant weren't built into the sales process. The aggressive sales effort failed magnificently because the sales people didn't fit the organizational culture based on relationships and trust.

In a small business, the entire company is the team. In larger organizations, work groups or departments can be teams. A real team wins and loses together, they train together, look out for each other, and build on each other's strengths. Unless the rewards are aligned with performance, and shared among the team, we propose that most companies don't actually have teams. That's okay, just don't call it a team when it's not one.

Most organizations actually have committees, which represent diverse interests (sales, R&D, manufacturing) the members of which may voluntarily support each other. But it's quite possible for some committee members to win while others lose. Don't try to "team build" a committee, which is like trying to paint water.

Once you hire an employee, the next step is to position them for long-term success. That involves training, the continual kind, not the six-hour kind.

Training and Development: If You Don't Build Your Team, Who Will?

My daughters take dance lessons all year long from Mrs. Miller at Applause Dance Academy. They practice their "triple *en dedans* pirouettes" to perform at competitions and annual recitals. Football players review films and practice all week long for a three-hour game. These training to performing ratios are high. What is your training to performing ratio?

Have you ever heard a business owner say that he or she didn't want to train employees because they would then leave for the competition? *The alternative to that is to have untrained employees who stay forever.* That won't work for any organization. The military, for example, is excellent at training their people to be promoted quickly as necessitated on the battlefield. What training will enable your people to take on more responsibility?

Training and development apply to all of your employees and managers. In fact, there is a clear progression of skills required to run and build a company. The front-line people require technical skills in sales and delivery while the back-office people require skills in administration. Managers require skills to oversee the technical people, monitor results, make decisions, and allocate resources. The leadership team requires strategic skills that look further ahead and into ambiguous and competitive environments with no clear parameters.

The leadership team is probably learning the most because what worked in the past is not guaranteed to work in the future. Everyone needs to be trained on how to think and act faster (Figure 5.3).

Figure 5.3 Levels of development

Wealth Building Blocks: Don't force everyone to take the same training programs. Train people at different levels within their similar groups. Blanket programs only smother growth.

Technical training

EMW Industrial successfully attracted new talent and grew its capacity because it hired brand new employees with no experience and put them through formal skills training and apprenticeship programs. It also helped that EMW focused on providing a very safe work environment so that parents knew their kids would be looked after on the job site.

Here is a list of proven technical training activities:

1. Apprenticeship and certifications that are accredited.
2. Formal college or university classes.
3. On-the-job training.
4. Practicing skills and passing a test.
5. High performers demonstrating their skills.

Technical training is about improving employee performance in order to increase results. The key strategy is to measure the individual employee's output on a regular basis. It's only by measuring results that you can determine if the training was successful.

Management development

A national franchisor trained its franchisees to operate and manage one location. As the local owner became more successful, they acquired more locations and suddenly had to manage multiple businesses. Management is about getting things done through other people. To improve your managers' skills, use these proven training activities:

1. Holding weekly meetings that discuss the prior week's results, what went well so you build on success, what could be improved, and setting goals for the next week.
2. Mentoring by senior people for career development.
3. Coaching for skill development such as presentations, communication, collaboration, and problem solving.
4. Work terms at other companies.

Strategic development

It is almost unnatural to think about the future further than you can see. Yet, that is what is required to successfully lead and grow your company.

Training to enhance your strategic skills includes:

1. Writing case studies about your own business growth, challenges, and successes, to codify the learning points and replicate success.
2. Testing all planned actions for strategic fit against your goals.
3. Examining all budget expenditures for strategic fit.

You can continually improve your strategic skills by examining the focus, direction, and alignment of your company's actions against your goals.

The worst training programs are often endorsed by human resources department and simply require people to attend a session and get their ticket stamped. There is neither testing of skills nor measuring of results. Often, there's not even a recognized need to fill, and HR has simply purchased, or created, a trendy—and often useless—program.

The best training programs improve measureable performance in the short-term.

Although you can measure the effectiveness of training, it's very difficult to measure the effectiveness of compensation. In fact, you may be wasting money by paying your people too much for the wrong things.

Compensation: Why You Don't Need to Be Scared of this Monster Anymore

Are you wasting money trying to motivate your employees by paying them too much? Money isn't a motivator, according to the legendary psychologist Frederick Herzberg,[1] but a lack of money leads to dissatisfaction. Yet, business owners tend to throw money at problems in a hope that the problem will go away. In terms of trying to fix an employee's poor attitude, the problem doesn't go away, just the money does. *If you give more money to an unhappy employee, you will have a wealthier, unhappy employee.*

Compensation is one of the easiest things to change in a business yet it's often very difficult to get right. That's because compensation is wrongly used to improve a variety of problems such as employee motivation, turnover, performance, and even culture. The keys to improving those problems are often based in the employees' relationships with their supervisors and peers, recognition, responsibility, the intrinsic value of the work itself, advancement, and personal growth, according to Herzberg.[2]

Wealth Building Blocks: If you pay an employee more money to motivate them, you just end up with a wealthier, unmotivated employee.

There are two common types of compensation that can be used either separately or together. *Fixed compensation* is what most employees receive, based on a predetermined wage or salary. *Variable compensation* fluctuates with performance and/or results. Examples include commissioned sales, performance bonuses for efforts, and results bonuses for achievements. As a business owner, all of *your* compensation is ultimately variable, based on your company's and employees' performance.

Aware of the fact that money isn't a motivator, one technology service company pays its sales professionals a high base salary and a low commission, thus minimizing significant fluctuations that exist in a project-based world. This mix is done to retain talent and provide them with a stable income that still rewards success.

---

[1] Herzberg's Motivation–Hygiene Theory,
http://www.netmba.com/mgmt/ob/motivation/herzberg/ Accessed April 25, 2015.
[2] Ibid.

There is no single formula of fixed and variable compensation that provides optimal retention and rewards. It depends on the nature of the work, the competitive environment, and the type of people that you need to perform in your business.

As a young college student, I was motivated to complete my education quickly and to have fun along the way. I worked on a construction crew that assembled farm storage Quonsets. These were steel buildings, typically 40 feet wide by 100 feet long, or larger. We were paid 100 percent variable compensation (by the square foot).

We worked hard. We were up at 5:00 am, on site by 6:00, and often worked until 7:00 pm or later. If it was daylight, and not raining, we were working. Even our customers—hardworking farmers—were impressed with our work ethic and productivity.

Our mobile factory generated a one-foot-wide steel semicircle that formed the wall and roof of the building and weighed a couple of hundred pounds. Our crew of four ran these rings into place, joined five rings together, and then lifted up the roof in five-foot sections with a crane. We were in great shape, physically and financially.

The Quonset company would not have received the same levels of production if we were paid a fixed salary. Who wants to run in the sun while carrying a steel ring if you get paid the same when you walk?

During a different summer, I worked on a survey crew for the highways department. We were paid a good fixed wage. We never ran and always allowed time for coffee breaks.

Compensation Keys:

- Total compensation should be in the middle of the range, or slightly higher, for the position and the local market conditions.
- If you have high turnover, you're probably not paying enough.
- A combination of high portion (70 percent or more) of fixed compensation along with variable compensation can allow an employee to receive more than 100 percent of average compensation while aligning the employee's performance with the company's objectives.
- Pay your employees as much as you need to and then do everything in your power to provide a rewarding career.

<u>Case Study</u>:

A services firm I worked for decided to boost sales performance by offering Cadillac—at the time worth about $60,000 each—to each of the top three performers the next year.

The result: The same level of overall sales and the same three top sales people finished in those positions the next year, but the company was $180,000 less profitable.

Don't use money to motivate your employees or solve their problems. In fact, there are many low or no-cost ways to deal with common employee problems. Read on.

Is the Tail Wagging the Dog? How to Overcome Common People Challenges.

"I can't fire him because then I would have to go back 'on the tools' and my business would shrink," one business owner told me several years ago.

"But you're losing business. He's practically stealing from you due to the loss in revenues and profits," I responded.

The owner shrugged. "I'm trapped," he sighed. "It takes years to train someone in our industry."

"No, it doesn't," was my reply. "It takes years to learn things by trial and error, without training, without systems or checklists, and without supervision or feedback. Otherwise, it takes a couple of weeks or months, depending on skill level and qualifications."

The owner built up his courage to deal with the tail-wagging-the-dog problem. Today, that same business has multiple locations, documented systems, formal training processes, and is highly profitable (Figure 5.4).

How much time do you and your managers spend responding to problems? What does this cost your business compared to spending that time *proactively* helping your customers and growing your business? Here is how you can calculate that: If you have annual revenues of $20 million, and if you and your managers spend 10 percent of your time on problems, then that costs you two million dollars a year of lost revenues (10 percent of your gross revenues). It's a simple calculation with a powerful

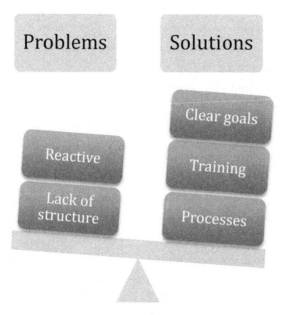

Figure 5.4 Problems vs. Solutions

result. Reducing problems, and the time spent solving them, creates more capacity to grow your business.

Problems also result in unhappy employees. If employees are stressed due to lack of clarity, lack of support, or a lack of information, that will negatively impact their performance. Stress is caused by a feeling that one doesn't know what will happen tomorrow and that one has no control over it. As an owner, you can address both of these factors.

Wealth Building Blocks: An unhappy employee will not create a happy customer. How happy are your employees?

Common complaints uttered about employees include the following items. Which apply to you now?

- They're not proactive and can't think for themselves.
- They keep making decisions without asking me.
- They always want more money.

- An employee left for a one-dollar-an-hour raise.
- They spend more time on social media than on business development.
- They don't want to do any paperwork and expect everything to be on the computer.
- They want a career path, training, feedback, and raises.
- They left for a larger company that has a pension plan and gave them a promotion.

The list goes on and on. The good news—and the bad news—is that your work environment is a product of your culture. Your culture is a product of your values and actions.

The key to dealing with problem employees is to "get corporate" and think and act like a much larger company with formal training, systems, and evaluations. That shift in your mindset will actually accelerate becoming a larger business.

I disagree with the adage about "hire for attitude and train the technical." Instead, hire for both attitude and technical skills. That way, you're three-quarters of the way to having a great employee.

The two basic performance problems are due to lack of skills or poor attitude. Robert Mager, a famous organizational development consultant, would ask the following question to determine which problem you had: "if you held a gun to their head, could they perform the task?"

If they could not perform the task, they had a skill deficiency, and required training or replacing. If they could perform but chose not to, then they had an attitude problem, and the employee should be coached (and removed if coaching did not work).

It is far more effective to prevent the causes of employee problems rather than applying contingent actions to solve the problems after they've occurred.

For additional advice on handling specific situations, see Alan's book, *"The Unofficial Guide to Power Managing*, published by IDG Books Worldwide, Inc.

Now that we've got your employees humming along, let's attract more customers.

CHAPTER 6

Marketing: How the Eternal Customer will Grow Your Business

Marketing isn't a department; it's everyone's responsibility, from front-line employees interacting with customers to back-office staff dealing with suppliers. Marketing is about increasing your customers' and prospects' awareness of the full range of value that you can provide to build your brand, attract customers, and increase revenues.

Marketing is the "place setting" for the sale. It creates the customer's awareness and need that your products and services fulfill.

Understanding Your Value: Numbers Speak Louder than Words

Let's assume that you and I are meeting for the first time, perhaps at a convention or meeting. In two or three sentences, describe what your business does?

Did you describe it from the perspective of your operations and skills? Did you say, "We sell things or fix things or build things?"

Business owners around the world have described their businesses based on their technical work. That's a mistake. Your value is based on the results—measurable results—that you create for your customers. The key is to measure. Most people don't do that.

Customers don't care what you do, they care about how they're better off after you do what you do.

This isn't just limited to business owners. It affects their advisors, too.

At the 2015 Million Dollar Consulting® Convention in Atlanta, only 58 percent of business consultants surveyed stated that they quantified the results that they generated for their clients. *Almost half don't measure their effectiveness.* So, how do you measure value?

Your value is not based on what you do. It's based on the economic and business results that you create for your clients and customers. You need to understand how your services flow through your customers to create economic and emotional results for their businesses.

Wealth Building Blocks: Your value is based on the quantifiable, tangible, and intangible results that you create for your customers.

Case Study: A computer service company was struggling to grow its business and increase profits. It described itself as a computer and network service company. That's very low on the economic ladder and labels them as a low-end commodity with many competitors. When they shifted their description and, more importantly, their self-perception, to being a high-value provider of technology that enabled their clients to accelerate growth and improve communication with their customers and employees, sales took off.

Here is an acronym for defining and quantifying your value: M E T R I C (Figure 6.1).

M = Measurable. This includes specific improvements in your customers' revenues, profits, customer acquisition, increased uptime, decreased downtime, speed, shipped-on-time, and on and on. It also includes subjective factors such as brand power, management team effectiveness, competitive position, and more. Just ask your customers, they will tell you.

E = Emotional. Logic makes us think and emotion makes us act. The highest value that you provide creates emotional value for your clients. If you prevent mechanical breakdowns and maximize asset health, like EMW Industrial does, then you provide executives and managers with feelings of control and confidence that their equipment will remain running, meet customer commitments, and deliver results on time and on budget.

T = Timely. Speed is as important, if not more important, than quality. A solution that is 80 percent correct tomorrow is, for many customers, greatly preferred over a solution that is 100 percent correct next month.

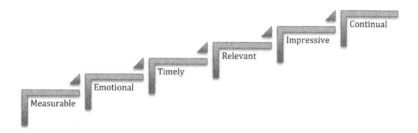

Figure 6.1 The METRIC model for quantifying value

R = Relevant. You know your technical expertise better than your customer knows your expertise. You can improve your customer's condition. Don't expect your customer to accurately self-diagnose. It's your job to be proactive and bold to specify how the customer will be better off.

I = Impressive. You have delivered significant and impactful results. Perhaps you undervalued them because "it was easy" or "it's what we always do." If you've improved inventory turnover by 300 percent at one company, tell everyone.

C = Continual. Show your customers that an investment in your products and services will generate continual improvements to their performance. Prove how your proactive maintenance can extend their asset life, increase return on assets, reduce breakdowns by 75 percent, and increase their capacity by 15 percent without any capital investment. Customers love annuities.

Applying the METRIC model will help you to understand the results that you create for your customers. This will have a very positive and powerful impact on all of your marketing activities. Let's start with building awareness.

Building Awareness: If You Don't Blow Your Own Horn, there will be No Music

How much do you invest in marketing, advertising, promotion, customer events, and other activities designed to generate sales each year? What is the return on your marketing investment?

The response rate on direct mail advertising is optimistically estimated at four percent. Billboard advertising is even lower. How can you attract new customers without using these expensive and inefficient tactics?

The key to blowing your own horn is to focus on people who want to hear your tune. Much of advertising budgets are wasted because they target everyone. By focusing your messages on your ideal buyer, you can dramatically increase your target market's awareness without wasting money on nonbuyers.

Let's talk about your marketing messages. If you listen to the radio or look at the newspaper, most of the advertisements feature products or services, some details, and prices. This is a no-win game with a discounting race to the bottom. However, if you write marketing copy in the format of a case study and use actual client results and comments, you will have more impact because your audience will be able to see itself benefitting from your help.

> **Wealth Building Blocks:** The most credible marketing message is a documentary style message, such as a case study, complete with hard numbers, and customer testimonials. Show them the numbers!

It's much more effective to discuss your customer's ROI on your services rather than your prices.

You can increase the effectiveness of your marketing and dramatically increase revenues by prioritizing your activities at your existing customers (and suppliers), your referral sources, and finally, at your prospects (Figure 6.2).

The traditional advertising model is designed to attract new customers. Yet this is a high-stakes, low-probability game. Marketing is much more effective when it's targeted at your existing customers who already know you and love you. They just don't know everything that you can do for them, yet. It's very likely that you would be able to increase your sales by 10 percent or more just by proactively calling your existing customers, inquiring about their business, and offering to help them.

Key Questions: Are your existing customers and clients fully aware of all the value that you can provide to them to help them be more successful? Are your employees similarly well informed about your offerings?

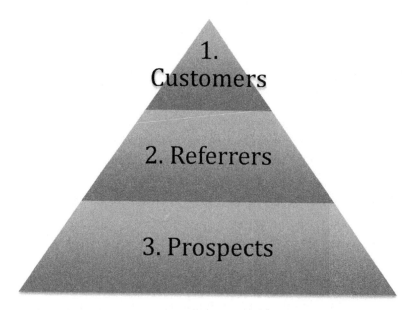

Figure 6.2 Targeting marketing for maximum ROI

The next most often ignored target market is your referral sources. Many established businesses have grown extensively from referrals. Yet, there is no formal process in place and no budget allocated to increase this valuable source of new business. The key steps are:

1. Identify important referral sources.
2. Meet with them at least quarterly to ask for referrals.
3. Proactively ask all of your customers for referrals.

My dentist, the good Dr. Blaine Friesen, has a sign in his reception area that says, "We welcome all referrals and new patients." Do you continually and automatically ask everyone for referrals? For more information on referrals, see Alan's book, *Million Dollar Referrals*, published by McGraw-Hill.

Your third priority, and the most expensive to attract, are new customers. The best way to attract new customers is to have your existing customers refer them to you. The prospects will be better educated and better qualified than many advertising respondents.

If you are going to invest money to attract new customers, make sure that you specify exactly who your ideal customer is, how you can help them, and how they can determine if they qualify as your customer.

Effective and low-cost activities to attract new customers include:

- Newsletters that provide valuable ideas and content.
- Videos that demonstrate customers using your products.
- Case studies that show success and enable a prospect to see themselves being helped.
- Think like a consultant and give away ideas on how to use your product or service.
- Have your best customers talk about you.
- Leverage your web presence to increase the reach and accessibility of your value.

For a great resource on how to utilize the Internet, see Alan and Chad Barr's book, *Million Dollar Web Presence*, published by Entrepreneur Press.

Building awareness isn't about advertising, it's about creating and distributing valuable content that makes you the main show, not just the ads.

Your two highest potential sources are existing products and services (with their strong endorsements and track records) to new customers, and new products and services to existing customers (with their belief in you and loyalty) (Figure 6.3).

Once you've attracted someone's interest to do business with you, then the negotiations begin. Next, you will see how to use the power of pricing to increase sales.

	Existing Customers	New Customers
New Products		
Existing Products		

Figure 6.3 Growth matrix

Source: Boston Consulting Group

The Power of Pricing: Give Your Customer Multiple Options to Say "Yes!"

Case Study:

Kevin Pare is a technology genius. He and his wife, Melanie Pare, own KSP Technology and help businesses leverage technology to increase their capacity, revenues, and profits. They provide corporate quality technology solutions for mid-market companies. KSP was innovative in providing several pricing options for their customers to select how pro-active they need their computer support to be. Their pricing options include bronze, silver, gold, diamond, and more! Customers love the flexibility and can move among the programs as their needs change. Their own business, KSP, is highly scalable because of their business model and technology.

How are you pricing your products and services? Check all that apply. Your choices include the following:

- Supply and demand, like diamonds and premier seats at sold-out concerts
- Competitors' pricing strategies, because you need to be competitive
- Cost based on your accountant's estimates (they're estimates, not facts) of direct labor, materials, overhead, and profit allocations according to accounting definitions of costs, not the real costs
- Time and materials where the meter is running and the supplier invoices get marked up and passed along, because we don't know how long it's going to take or what it's going to cost, like a home renovation gone bad
- Industry standards, such as hourly rates for professional service firms
- Guesswork

All of the above pricing models—which are highly utilized by small and large companies alike—are costing you millions in lost revenues, creating a perception that you are a commodity, and driving your customers to your competitors.

Your pricing needs to represent your value to your customers (Figure 6.4).

Here is my pricing formula: $P = Q \times R \times S \times T \times U$

Price = Quality × Relevance × Speed × Time × Uniqueness

Quality is about your product/service and your customer's entire interaction with you, including ordering, receiving, storing, implementing, and even paying you.

Relevance is how effective your solution is at creating results. Computer manufacturers do this by allowing you to configure the specifications. Auto dealers have computer "configurators" in their stores.

Speed is about your responsiveness in all aspects of ordering and delivery. Mid-market companies have a huge advantage over larger companies in this area. In fact, as we wrote about previously, speed can trump quality.

Time is how long your product lasts before it needs to be replaced.

Uniqueness depends on how customizable you are and how many competitors you have.

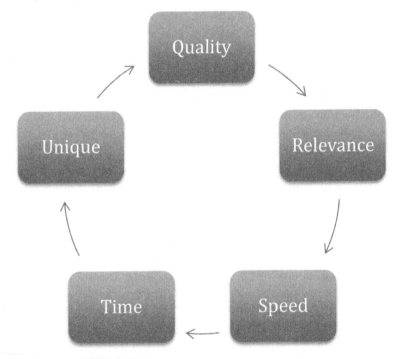

Figure 6.4 Pricing formula

These factors represent your value to your customers. You may have some different factors. The key is to use these to drive your pricing. Therefore, continually communicating your value in all of your marketing activities is critical to increasing your pricing power.

Let's use a simple example. Hamburgers range from 99 cents at a fast food joint to 25 dollars (or more for Kobe beef) at a high-end restaurant. The basic components are similar. Yet, the taste and overall experience will be significantly different due to the quality of the ingredients (ground chuck and tenderloin compared to ground beef), whether you're in your car and in a rush, and if you're looking for sustenance vs. delight, whether you're served or have to wait in line. You have options when acquiring a hamburger.

Do you give your customers options when they are attempting to purchase your goods and services?

Many businesses give their customer one price: take it or leave it. The odds aren't stacked in your favor. If you give your customer three options, that stacks the odds for you. Options turn a "one price" yes/no, 50/50 purchase decision into a "three price" yes/yes/yes/no, 75/25 favorable purchase decision. Giving three price options increase your odds of success by at least 50 percent.

You can leverage any or all of the variables in our pricing formula to create options. You probably won't need to adjust them all, especially if your quality is consistently high. In fact, many businesses offer only one level of quality: "our best!"

One of the most overlooked but powerful variables is speed. Mid-market companies can differentiate themselves from larger, slower competitors by focusing on speed. Most customers want solutions as quickly as possible. Your large customers probably need to customize your products or services on short notice. You can build a huge business by focusing on speed and charging different prices for different levels of responsiveness.

Wealth Building Blocks: Customizing your value to meet your customer's needs gives you more pricing power because you can give your customers more choices.

The most common options for mid-market companies include creating bundles of your value at three different levels: bronze, silver, and gold.

Figure 6.5 outlines how to maximize each of these three factors.

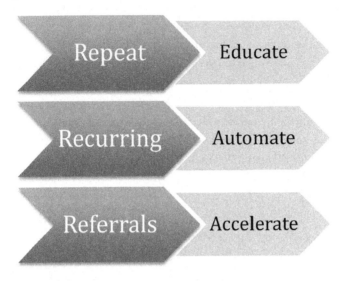

Figure 6.5 The three Rs of increasing sales

Options will make your customers happier because they will have more control in the process. Happier customers will refer more people to you. Let's see how we can put your referrals on auto-pilot.

The Three Rs: Your Best Marketing Doesn't Cost Any Money

In grade school, we learned about reading, writing, and arithmetic. The three fastest ways to increase your revenues are also based on the three Rs: repeat business, recurring business, and referrals.

> **Wealth Building Blocks:** The most effective ways to increase sales are by focusing on repeat business, recurring business, and referrals. And they don't cost any money!

Repeat business

You purchase groceries and gas every week . . . probably from the same store and gas station. We are, after all, creatures of habit. If your dentist and hair stylist can book your next appointment before you leave, how can you do the same for your customers?

The keys to building repeat business are to proactively and continually educate your existing customers (and staff) about your full suite of products, services, and value. Everyone should know what you are capable of doing.

Your customers don't want to be sold to; they want to be helped. And, they prefer to be helped proactively instead of waiting until something goes wrong or they run out of fuel. The best way to become proactive is to think and act like a consultant who shares ideas instead of a manufacturer of things or a supplier of hourly technicians.

A product company can proactively analyze its customers purchasing data and recommend how the customer can order more while reducing costs. According to Jim Grew, an operations expert, a paint supply company told its industrial customer that they could save money by ordering larger 55 gallon paint drums instead of smaller five gallon pails. Everyone was happy and more profitable.

How can you inform your customers of all of the ways that you can increase their success?

Recurring business

Recurring business is repeat business on steroids because it has been automated. My drycleaner, Belgian Cleaners, automatically shows up every Thursday morning for their weekly pickup. They also show up with dog treats for Lola, our chief moral officer. The entire household is very well informed of the dry cleaner's arrival due to Lola's enthusiastic barking.

A fuel supply company remotely monitors its customers' inventory levels and automatically dispatches trucks to fill the tanks. A distributor has its computer talk to its customers' computers and remotely monitors inventory levels. When the customer sells out its inventory below its reorder point, the computer triggers an order.

You can increase recurring business by automating sales and delivery. This can be based on timing or frequency, as our weekly drycleaner has done. Or it can be automated based on inventory levels. Although your team is visiting your customers and topping up their inventory, you may want to ask them what else is going on in their business.

How can you automate and increase your customers' buying habits?

Referrals

In my experience, over 80 percent of businesses have grown from referrals. The most surprising statistic is most of those businesses don't spend any money on referrals and don't have a formal referral system.

If you refer your friend to a business that you deal with, you actually benefit three people: the business receiving the new customer, your friend because they have a trusted company to deal with, and yourself because you've strengthened your relationship with your friend and the other business. Knowing the emotional power of referrals, asking for them should become much easier.

The process is simple. Ask your customer the following: "Who do you know who would also benefit from the same value that we've provided to you?" The language is very important so that it is easy for them to identify specific people.

Next, ask them to introduce you. That may be done via a phone call, an email introduction, a lunch, or even a joint meeting. Once you've been referred, let the referring person know that you've contacted the referral. They appreciate knowing that you are taking care of their friend.

When will you ask your regular customers for referrals?

As the referrals start rolling in, it's time to finalize the sale and get the prospect to sign on the dotted line.

Sales: How to Get the Customer to Sign on the Dotted Line

The young sales manager looked at me and complained, "I'm spending so much time writing up quotes that I don't have time to follow up." He pulled open a file drawer overflowing with old quotes. We added them up and they totaled more than the prior year's annual sales. "Wow," he said, "how do I close these deals?"

There are two kinds of sales: proactive and reactive. Proactive sales occur when your sales force goes out, finds business, closes business, and gets paid for closing. Reactive sales occur when your customer calls or emails, places an order, and then you deliver.

What percentage of your sales is proactive or reactive (Figure 6.6)?

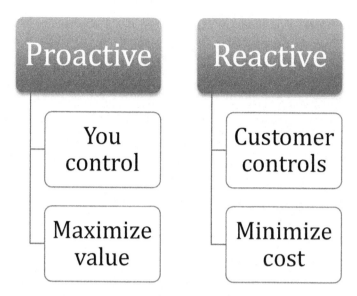

Figure 6.6 Who is driving your sales?

Many companies grew organically because they were simply good at delivering their products or services. There often were no formal marketing or sales resources in place. The phone rang, an order was taken, it was delivered, and cash was collected. That process drove organic growth.

That doesn't work anymore.

Your customers have access to your and your competitors' information. Your customers control more of the buying process. As your company focuses on future growth, you need to proactively control—and increase—sales so that you can control production, cash flow, and your destiny. The best way to do is to proactively ask your customers how you can contribute to their success, and then offer to help them increase their success even more.

While the reactive business will keep coming in (hopefully), you need to apply the following process to both your proactive and reactive opportunities.

The steps are the following:

1. Take control of the sales or order conversation by asking this question: "So that I may help you best, is it okay if I ask you a few questions?"

2. Proactively assess the specified request or opportunity in terms of the desired results.

3. Clarify the customer's needs and wants by asking questions about logical outcomes and emotional benefits.

4. Quantify the value of those outcomes and results. This consultative conversation will differentiate you from competitors and elevate you above commodity status.

5. Create options for your customer to maximize their results and thus increase their ROI from purchasing with you.

6. Provide your customer with at least two options so they have a choice of yeses.

7. Offer to ship today. Speed has significant value.

8. Give the customer a deadline.

9. Offer them an incentive for accepting quickly. This does not require a discount. You can offer something of value to them that has little or no cost to you such as faster response time or customization.

10. Ask for the sale by saying, "Which option maximizes your ROI?"

> **Wealth Building Blocks:** Treating all sales opportunities—whether they were originally a proactive or a reactive order—with the same process of quantifying the customer's results will help to maximize the sale.

Have you ever lost a great customer whom you thought was loyal and safe? Many sales people (and business owners) ignore their largest customers because it's a bigger rush to land a new customer. Don't ignore your existing customers. In fact, focus your sales efforts on your existing customers first, and then ask them for referrals. Then, focus on the warm referrals.

Finally, make sure that your sales people are compensated for results. If they're paid just for showing up, they're not sales people, they are glorified order takers. After all, as a business owner, you are paid for results. Make sure that you're not the only person in the place with that privilege.

The young sales manager with the pile of quotes sorted the quotes by size, ranked the largest ones, picked up the phone, asked for their orders, and had a record month.

How many sales are hiding in someone's file drawer or computer folder?

The best sales people don't sell stuff; they help to increase their customers' successes. That's an honorable role to perform.

Now that you've attracted prospects and converted them to customers, it's time to collect the cash and use those funds to accelerate your growth and wealth.

PART 3

Build Your Business Wealth

CHAPTER 7

From the Vault: Financial Strategies to Accelerate Profits, Valuation, and Wealth

Flash reports: Why Waiting for Your Month-End Financial Statements is Like Reading an Obituary

"Dad, how many more miles? Are we there yet?"

As a parent, I can now answer that question by saying, "Check your iPhone, what does Google Maps say?" Now, they tell me how many more miles remain. So does the car's navigation system, but it's fun to teach the kids how to figure things out for themselves.

Flash reports are like your car's GPS and tell you where you are, in real time, every day. Flash reports also empower employees to measure—and improve—their performance. You don't want, and in fact can't wait, for the month-end financial statements to tell you the most important data about your company. If you receive your month-end reports by the middle of the next month, some of that information is already six weeks old and you still don't know what's happening today.

Financial statements are useful as lagging indicators because they tell you what happened in the past (like an obituary) from a financial perspective. They are not useful to improve financial performance in real time. That's why flash reports need to measure and report—on a daily basis—three critical areas of your business: the sales pipeline, production volumes, and cash.

Wealth Building Blocks: Tracking three flash metrics every day—sales pipeline, production, and cash—will empower your team to dramatically and continually improve performance.

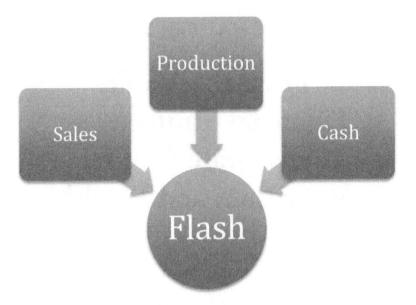

Figure 7.1 Flash reports

Tracking these, even if it's on a sticky note or white board, will generate great ideas from the front-line people on how to improve the numbers. The best ideas, and true innovation, come from the front lines. They don't come from head office or weeklong strategy retreats (Figure 7.1).

The best way to improve performance in a critical area is to report on that performance every day, compare good days vs. bad days, and continually share what is working on the good days to ensure that all days keep getting better. In fact, there's something about human nature that says we want to know the score. That's why we always kept score while playing street hockey or stickball. Keeping track of production allows everyone to win as they improve performance and results.

Look for the distinctions in failing to meet expectations and surpassing expectations, and eliminate the former while exploiting the latter.

Many companies start by measuring one factor daily. Some examples and ideas are shown in Table 7.1.

All companies have internal best practices that are likely invisible. Flash reports help to identify areas of strong performance so hidden best practices can be shared across other departments or divisions.

The sales pipeline is important because it shows business that is sold and promised to customers. In other words, it includes only real numbers.

Table 7.1 Daily flash metrics

Industry	Daily Flash Metric
Service company	Billable time—improved from 45% to over 80%.
Construction firm	Daily project hours—improved project management and completion.
Industrial company	Safety statistics and near-misses where all infractions had to be called in to the CEO within one hour. —Resulted in significant improvement in safety awareness and culture.
Consulting firm	Number of marketing calls and actions per day—resulted in new client projects and revenues.

This does not include projected or estimated sales based on arbitrary and artificial numbers as these create a false sense of security that results in busts when the sales don't materialize, according to Colleen Francis, author of *Nonstop Sales Boom, published by* AMACOM, 2015.

The production volumes show actual speed, quality, and results. *This allows you to divide the sales pipeline by the production speed to determine how many days, weeks, or months of work you have right now.* That's a real number. How long is your production pipeline?

All businesses, especially high-growth businesses, need cash to survive. If you generate your own cash, then you can fund your own growth. The formula for cash is: Cash = Margin × Volume × Velocity. You can determine your cash burn rate—how much cash you consume per day or week—and see how long you can fund your own operations. Ideally, you have access to short-term cash that will increase your capacity for growth.

Cash is an important part of your overall working capital. Next, we'll show you how working capital improvements can accelerate profits and build business wealth.

Working Capital: How Improving Your "Total Days to Cash" will Fuel Your Business

How have you funded your business growth? Did you increase your borrowing, inject your own money into your business, lean on your suppliers, or beg your customers to pay you more quickly? Those are all valid sources of cash. I want to show you how you can generate more cash from internal operations and processes.

Many mid-market companies have successfully grown their businesses by selling more to larger customers. These larger customers often take longer to pay. As CFOs of global companies conserve cash by slowing down payments to you, their suppliers, that causes ripples that feel like tsunamis to growing companies hungry for cash.

In fact, many profitable companies that are growing quickly will run out of cash long before they run out of profits. That's why focusing on the "P&L" or income statement is very dangerous. It's the working capital items on your balance sheet that create—or consume—cash. These items include cash itself, raw material inventory, accounts receivable, accounts payable, lines of credit, and other deferred liabilities. However, to really accelerate your "Total Days to Cash," we want to focus on all of the inputs that initially consume, and ultimately create, cash.

> **Wealth Building Blocks:** For capital to be working, it needs to move . . . quickly. The keys to strong working capital are speed and leverage.

Let's look at this model that shows the inputs and eventual outputs of your cash cycle. It looks at the initial cash outlays for wages and overheads as soon as you turn on the lights in the morning (Figure 7.2).

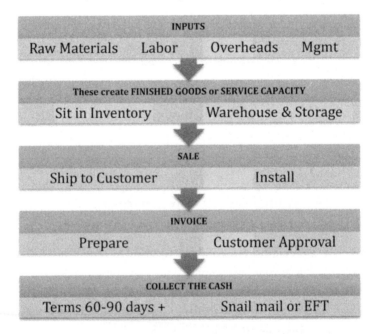

Figure 7.2 The "Total Days to Cash" cycle

Many businesses use "Days Sales Outstanding" (DSO) to measure cash flow speed. It has limited usefulness because it doesn't start until an invoice has been prepared. If it takes your company 30 days to manufacture, 45 days to sell, and 15 days to invoice, then you've already got 90 days into the cycle, *yet DSO shows one day* because it just starts when you send the invoice. That's a huge distortion of reality.

That's why I recommend "Total Days to Cash" which includes the original payroll, raw material purchases, and overheads that you paid for weeks (or months) ago.

Using this framework, what is your "Total Days to Cash" number? How can you improve it?

Here are five ways to improve your working capital.

1. Don't use cash (or your operating line) to purchase long-term assets such as equipment. Use leasing or term debt as this matches the financing terms to the asset's useful life. This leaves cash for operations.

2. Focus on speed everywhere throughout the process, including information flow, paperwork, and physical flow. This is where supply chain gurus have made a positive impact on mid-market companies. For example, order materials and supplies in smaller batches as you need them, so you're not wasting time storing and moving materials. Caution: Apply common sense and beware of the fanatics who are sixth-degree black belts in some artificial model that a consultant created to make money.

3. Don't store raw materials if you don't have to. Push that role to your suppliers, just as the auto manufacturers have done with just-in-time inventory with their suppliers.

4. Ensure that you have an adequate and margined operating line of credit for continued growth. If you are growing at 25 percent or more per year, it will be difficult for a nonmargined line of credit to keep up. Margined means that the limit fluctuates up and down with the level of clean accounts receivable (less than 60 or 90 days old) and inventory. You might obtain more than 75 percent if your customers are publicly traded or government.

5. Measure how long everything takes and continually try to do it faster. When I owned a drywall construction company, we could issue an invoice in 10 minutes. We asked our customers to pay us in 10 days because we were a start-up and needed to generate as much cash as possible.

Working capital is about speed and leverage. In addition to the operating line of credit, let's discuss financing your business with other people's money.

Financing the Future: The Good, the Bad, and the Ugly of Using Other People's Money

Has your accountant asked you if you wanted to minimize taxes and did you agree? If so, shame on both of you! Next, you probably heard your banker say, "Sorry but we can't lend you more money because you're not profitable enough." Welcome to the accountant–banker dilemma.

Your goal as a business owner, and your accountant's goal, should be to *maximize your after-tax cash flow to build your wealth.* That's a huge difference from minimizing taxes.

Wealth Building Blocks: Minimizing short-term taxes is a terrible strategy if you want to grow your business and build wealth.

Here is an example to prove this point. Feel free to use your own numbers and tax rates here. Better yet, ask your accountant to crunch these numbers for you.

Let's assume that you have $1,000,000 in profits and that you want to keep growing your business. Your accountant says, "We can eliminate any taxes by declaring and paying a bonus to you (or your holding company)." If you accept this, then this doesn't actually eliminate the tax; it defers or shifts that tax burden from your operating company to your holding company or to you personally. And, you actually need to fund that $1,000,000 payment with cash. The entity receiving the payment will need to pay tax (but probably next year, based on tax deferral!). Accountants are famous for deferring tax. This cash could be put to better uses. Let me show you a better way.

If you have $1,000,000 in profits and pay out $1,000,000 in a bonus to yourself, you've got a net profit of zero and therefore zero tax. If you leave all of the money in your company, and assuming that you pay tax at 30 percent, then you will pay $300,000 of tax and have $700,000 of cash left over. This also means that you will have added $700,000 of equity into the retained earnings on your balance sheet.

Bankers don't lend from your income statement. They lend from your balance sheet. Bankers do this by applying a simple ratio called "debt-to-equity" to set a limit on how much you can borrow. For a mature, growing business, this debt-to-equity is typically set at two-to-one. In other words, for every dollar of equity you retain in your business, the bank will allow you to borrow—in total—two dollars.

In the above example, you added $700,000 to equity. Now, you can borrow up to $1,400,000 more, using the two-to-one ratio. Let's assume that you borrow $1.4 million and invest in inventory. If you turn over inventory four times per year at a gross margin of 50%, then you will have generated $11.2 million (4 × $1.4m/50%) in sales. The cost of sales will be $5.6 million (4 × $1.4 million). Thus, you will net $5.6 million in pretax income (assuming no other costs), and $3.92 million in after-tax income (at 30% tax).

In other words, you paid $300,000 in tax, left the excess money in your company, borrowed against the retained earnings, and generated an additional $3.92 million in after-tax profit. And, you still had the first $700,000 to use in other ways to drive your growth.

$3,920,000/$300,000 is an ROI of 1,307 percent. That's not bad for paying $300,000 in tax. Conservatively, even one-half of that gain would be more than 650 percent ROI.

Wealth Building Blocks: Minimizing taxes will reduce your borrowing power, hurt your business growth, and seriously reduce your long-term wealth. Pay the tax and invest in your future success.

Good debt includes the following:

1.   Operating lines of credit to bridge the gap between paying suppliers and collecting accounts receivable.

2. Long-term debt to acquire assets such as land, buildings, and equipment that will last three or more years. Long-term debt may require personal guarantees to the bank. This has its limits so negotiate carefully.

3. Leases—either operating or capital—to finance the acquisition of equipment lasting less than five years. Leases often don't require personal guarantees.

Doug Yaremko, associate vice president at a global bank, says that retained earnings allow banks to lend more money to help fund their clients' growth.

Interest rates are at historically low levels. Good debt represents an excellent way to grow your business and build your wealth.

The best way to measure your business wealth is from your financial statements.

Financial Reporting: It's About the Past, the Present, and the Future

Is your accounting department focused on providing useful and timely reports for your management team or are they focused on preparing historical compliance reports for bankers, government, and other third parties? The former will increase your profits and the latter is just an expense to be minimized. Which description fits you?

How would you feel if you had to publicly report your quarterly results for the last quarter and state your goals for the next quarter? If this terrifies you, you're not alone. In fact, many business owners hide critical financial information from some (or all) of their management team. How can those managers be held accountable for results if they don't know the results? It's time to get corporate and share your critical information.

A good accounting department will balance its time and generate useful information about the past, the present, and the future. If they are taking two to three weeks to generate last month's financial reports about the past, they won't have much time to focus on flash reports showing the present situation or updating future plans to give you confidence about where you are going.

That's scary. That's like driving forward with your windshield covered up and only seeing where you've been in the rear view mirror.

Wealth Building Blocks: The most useful financial information shows exactly where you are now and where you are going to be in the near future, just like a good navigation system in your car.

The Past

Historical financial information in standard accounting format summarizes and distorts reality because it's formatted for third parties, not managers. Managers need detail—the gold—that's hidden in that historical data. Ask your CFO for the following information on a monthly basis:

- Sales by line item or major category to show patterns and identify opportunities to predict—and improve—the future.
- Gross profit dollars and gross margin percentage by product or service line, by customer, and by location.
- Contribution margin by discrete product and service to show your true winners and losers. Often, a loser can be turned into a winner by decreasing the price and dramatically increasing total sales as the product becomes more competitive.
- Aged accounts receivable by customer and sales person and ensuring that payment terms are being followed.

Even simple accounting systems can create this information. A good accounting system will make you money. You should receive this information by 10th of every month. When do you receive it?

The Present

Managers need to see key metrics on sales, production, and cash flow every day. The flash report should be on your computer every day by 9:00 a.m. It's that simple, and that important.

The Future

The most difficult thing to predict in any company is future sales. Just ask any public company CEO or CFO. Public companies get rewarded or punished for hitting or missing their targets, respectively. Your company may not report quarterly results to the public, but you do need the corporate discipline and focus to set and pursue targets. More importantly, you need to compare your results against your plans. That way, you continually get smarter. Without goals and plans, you're not in control.

Future reporting builds on the patterns and trends observed in the historical and flash reports. Specifically, you need the following information:

- Rolling 13-week sales projections, production schedule, and cash flows. If you can see it coming, you can control it, and you can improve it.
- Brief projections of future cost drivers such as labor rates, overhead, and interest rates. (What if interest rates climb to 5 or 10 percent? These are simple calculations that help you to stress test your business.)
- Rolling 13-month financial projections showing key ratios on your balance sheet, income statement, and cash flow. You never want your banker advising you of covenant violations after they occur.
- Major economic trends impacting your customers and suppliers. What if oil stayed below US$50 per barrel?

The goal of future reporting isn't total accuracy, since you'll never hit every aspect of your plan. The goal is to increase your confidence and control about the future.

Wealth Builder Financial Dashboard

Use Table 7.2 to organize key financial information.

Table 7.2 Wealth builder dashboard

PAST (monthly)	PRESENT (daily)	FUTURE (monthly)
Sales Details: Sales by line Sales by customer Gross profits by line Gross profits by customer Contribution by product	Sales Pipeline: Dollars sold Weeks of work	Sales goals and status (on target, ahead, behind)

PAST (monthly)	PRESENT (daily)	FUTURE (monthly)
Sales Trends by Line: Customer sales Trends Costing trends	Production: Volume Speed	Next Quarter: Rolling 13-week reports
Balance sheet ratios Income statement ratios	Cash: Total Days to Cash Aged accounts receivable Aged accounts payable	Next Year: Rolling 13-month reports

Now that you have your financial information organized, let's discuss how your management team can use this information.

Financial Management Best Practices: What Your Financial Statements Aren't Telling You

(Note: There is some excellent, technical, financial process information below. You may want your financial people to read this section and discuss it with them.)

A banker called and said, "I've got this great client who wants to grow his business. His customers love him, he takes great care of his employees, but he needs a financial expert to help him grow his business." Little did I know that this one call was going to turn into seven years of excitement.

When I showed up at the business, I discovered that five administrative people were sharing a single-user version of QuickBooks. They took turns working in the system, yelling to each other to log out. I was shocked. Before I left that first day, I made sure that they purchased a multiuser license and everyone was instantly more productive.

How strong are your financial management practices? Does everyone have the information they need to run and grow their business?

There are four best practices to financial management: information, reporting, planning, and decision-making (Figure 7.3).

Information is the relevant data often buried or invisible in your organization. The first step is to track the relevant information. How do you know what's relevant? Ask your front-line people what they do all day and measure that. Then, ask your managers what they need to know to improve production of the first factor and generate that information.

Figure 7.3 Financial management process

All of this information should be automated or, ideally, on a comput-
erized system, such as an Enterprise Resource Planning (ERP) system, that
includes all sales, operations, and financial data—yes, the Flash Data—in
one place. You can turn a basic accounting system into an ERP type of
system by recording key activities as one-dollar items in your income
statement and then set up a contra account to offset this item.

For example, if your service people deliver 1,000 hours on Tuesday, then you would record 1,000 in the Hours Delivered account by date and negative 1,000 in a Contra Metrics account. The net is zero and won't affect your income statement or tax calculations. Next, you could record how many hours were billed using the same process. Now, you have a powerful metric showing billing efficiency: hours billed/hours delivered. A full scale ERP system will record this data by date, technician, project, customer, manager, and location.

When your system records all of this information, it can generate reports that organize and summarize data that is relevant for your managers. Different people at different levels get different information. The major opportunity is to use real-time information to monitor sales and operations as those factors create financial results. If you just use financial information, which is a lag indicator, you're missing reality and you can't improve results.

Real-time metrics should be available daily. Monthly financial statements should be ready by the 10th of the next month, at the latest.

Some business owners balk at the large cost of a good ERP system. Yet, its cost is equivalent to a few people, and these people are probably already performing redundant (and delayed) data input. Most ERP systems pay for themselves in a couple of years. Some pay for themselves in one year by saving on project losses. You want to acquire a system that is essentially set up for your industry and requires general ledger account mapping. Beware of highly powerful systems that are entirely customized from scratch. Those are expensive messes waiting to happen.

A good ERP system will maximize the value of your business because information is a foundation for growth.

Planning is simply the process of setting goals and then comparing your actual results to those goals. The purpose isn't to hit your goals as you will usually be over or under them. The purpose is to make you smarter—every day—by identifying what is and isn't working to your expectations.

Decision-making is best done in real time with accurate information that shows your actual results against your expected results. Without a baseline, you don't know whether you're doing well or improving. Comparing to the same period last year is useful only if you know why things happened in both periods. Comparing to plans is the best way to grow your business.

> **Wealth Building Blocks:** A good information system will provide managers with real-time information that improves their decision-making and drives results.

The four steps of information gathering, reporting, planning, and decision-making are the foundation for great financial management. The company mentioned at the start of the chapter grew revenues over 300 percent by following those steps.

> ## Case Study: Morsky Group of Companies
> Lorne Schnell, president of Morsky Management Group, advises: "With a high growth company comes extreme demands for capital and people. Strategies around capital requirements are easy – get as much working capital as you can, as fast as you can, at whatever rate you can get...Develop strong relationships with various lenders; talk to anyone and everyone, and cement relationships with those that are most supportive...about your business prospects. The same goes for people, although this can be challenging ...But you could make the case that THE key to leadership is promoting the core purpose and core values of the company in the marketplace, and attracting talent that will thrive in a high growth environment."

Now that you have financial information to control your business, you can focus on maximizing growth and building your wealth.

CHAPTER 8

Five Secrets to Building Your Business Wealth: How Firing Yourself Can Make You Rich

Personal Balance Sheet: You're Richer Than You Think

My grandmother lived past 102 years. At the age of 93, she was still riding her three-wheeled bike down Main Street to pick up groceries from the local co-op store, her Toronto Blue Jays ball cap holding her white hair firmly in place. The buses and trucks slowly followed her as she held her lane. She told me many times, usually after she spent the afternoon in her vegetable garden, "If you don't have your health, you don't have anything."

Many business owners make more significant contributions to their communities and their economies than the high-priced, multimillion dollar professional athletes whom we watch on TV. Yet, the athletes take much better care of themselves—mentally and physically—than the business owners do. In fact, some business owners take better care of their cars than they do of themselves, their families, or their personal relationships. Your health is your most important personal and business asset.

> **Wealth Building Blocks:** The main economic driver for your business and your family is your health. Are you in peak condition?

In business, your balance sheet represents what you own (assets) and what you owe (liabilities) at a specific point in time. The difference—assets minus liabilities—is your equity. The assets are used to generate

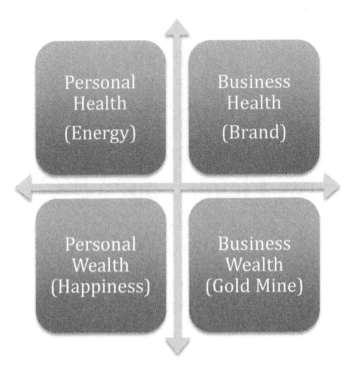

Figure 8.1 The wealth builder cycle

the results that show up on your income statement and that create cash. The liabilities are hopefully productive leverage that allow you to create faster results.

This applies to your personal life as well. Your main assets are your health and your wealth. Your health includes your energy, creativity, passion, relationships, and disposition, and these *all unite to create your wealth* (Figure 8.1).

To increase your personal health:

- Get at least 30 minutes of exercise each day. Our bodies are made to move, not to sit at a desk or computer all day. Go for a walk. Putting your feet on your desk is not exercise.
- Eat healthy. All calories are not created equally. A mixture of proteins, high-fiber carbohydrates, and healthy fats like fish oils and olive oil will give you much more energy and will protect your heart, according to Harley Pasternak, physical trainer and health advisor to the stars. Allow yourself a one-day exception every week to find the ultimate cheeseburger.

- Positivity is priceless. Surround yourself with positive people who support and encourage you. We can choose our friends, so choose carefully. We can't choose our family, so minimize contact with negative people who suck the energy out of life. There is an entire discipline of "positive psychology" which posits that the way we talk to ourselves determines our success.[1]
- Utilize your talents and strengths in productive ways: set big goals, get things done, and then reward yourself. This positive cycle will keep your energy and momentum high. We're not here to stick our toes in the water, but rather to make waves.
- Keep your health checkups current so that you can prevent or catch major health problems before they undermine your strength.
- Manage your two major health risks: waste circumference and stress levels. Get professional help when needed. (You have to embrace positive stress and minimize dangerous stress.)

To strengthen your business health and brand:

- Ask your customers what the best results are that you've created for them.
- Continually strengthen your brand by quantifying your results, proving your ROI to your customers, and using those specific metrics to attract new and larger customers. Don't be afraid to "blow your own horn."
- Have your customers do your marketing for you in terms of referrals and word-of-mouth advertising. Their referral will be much more effective than likes on social media. This is the heart of "business evangelism."

To build your business wealth:

- Set your prices based on the unique value you provide and the results that you create for your ideal customers.

---

[1] For example, see Dr. Martin Seligman's *Learned Optimism*.

- Create and build up your cash flow where cash comes from: Profit Margin × Volume of Sales × Velocity of Payment.
- Continually maximize the profitability of your company so as to strengthen its strategic value.
- Use debt and leverage *wisely* to accelerate growth and profits.
- Don't minimize taxes; maximize after-tax cash flows.

To develop perpetual personal wealth and happiness:

- Wealth is about discretionary time and the mindset to enjoy it. It is about an abundance mentality, not a scarcity mentality.
- Use positive daily affirmations and self-talk, as per Martin Seligman, the father of positive psychology. Not only are we "what we eat," we are also "what we tell ourselves."
- Keep things in perspective. We're on a huge chunk of rock that is rotating at 1,037 mph[2] and is traveling through space at approximately 66,000 mph[3] around an exploding star. Whether you realize it or not, you have faith.

By taking actions every day to strengthen your personal and business health, you will build both your business and personal wealth.

Since the purpose of your business is to provide you with wealth, and we define wealth as discretionary time, we're going to explore this further.

True Wealth is Discretionary Time: If You Have to be there, You Don't Have a Business, You Have a Job

When I first started my solo consulting practice, I came home at 11:00 p.m. after working late on a project but couldn't unlock my front door. The key wouldn't open the lock. Frustrated, I kept trying the same key,

---

[2]Dr. Sten Odenwald, http://image.gsfc.nasa.gov/poetry/ask/a10840.html accessed on May 17, 2015.
[3]Callister, Jeffrey. *Brief Review in Earth Science*. New York: Prentice Hall, 1990: 38. (Calculation: 29.77 km/s /1.625 km/mile × 3,600 sec/hour = approx. 66,000 mph)

since I knew I was at the right house. My wife heard the commotion and let me in. She took one look at the key I was holding. "You're trying to unlock the house with your office key," she coolly advised. That was the day I realized that nothing good happens from working late. I always made it home for dinner after that.

Prior to my consulting practice, I worked as a controller for an oil and gas subsidiary of a government corporation, and commuted two days per week to Calgary, a one-hour flight each way. After two years, I had built up enough Westin points to take my wife on a free trip to Ixtapa, Mexico. Since we were newly married, we were very excited about this free trip, and booked it for March. As March approached and I realized the enormity of my workload combined with business owners wanting their financial statements and advice, I had to cancel the trip. My wife understood. However, I stopped traveling, forgot to renew my Westin points, and lost them all.

I learned the hard way that a business is like a black hole with infinite gravity to consume all of the time and energy that you offer. The business will never be satisfied. Or, so I thought. I was wrong.

In his great book called *The Goal*, Eli Goldratt talks about the theory of constraints. It's not about increasing volume, he says, to increase production. It's about decreasing batch size to increase speed and thereby increase volume.

In other words, we need to sprint to achieve our goals as quickly as possible. We can't pursue 10 goals at a same time. We need to pursue one or two goals, achieve them, reward ourselves, reflect on our successes, and then repeat the process.

Wealth Building Blocks: Discretionary time comes from pursuing and achieving goals in sprints and then taking time to enjoy your results and recharge your batteries.

You can increase your discretionary time in both your business and your personal life. This is very important because you actually have only one life. The same principles apply to both parts of your life (Figure 8.2).

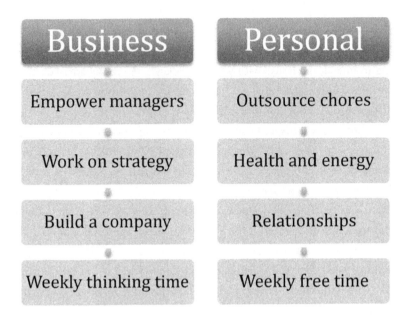

Business	Personal
Empower managers	Outsource chores
Work on strategy	Health and energy
Build a company	Relationships
Weekly thinking time	Weekly free time

Figure 8.2 Creating discretionary time

What would you do if you had the privilege, like a tenured professor, of taking a sabbatical for an entire year? Most business owners would relax and unwind in two weeks, create ideas for new ventures in the next week or two, and be chomping at the bit to start implementing their plans by week five, at the latest. An annual sabbatical is totally unrealistic—and unnecessary—for most business owners. What you need is a weekly sabbatical (popularized by Alan Weiss in his trademarked video series, The Weekly Sabbatical).

In the days of yore, professionals took Wednesday afternoons off to play golf. Although I don't consider golf a sabbatical in any way, a regular break from work is good for the mind, the body, and the balance sheet.

In his book *The Power of Habit*, Charles Duhigg states that we all have habits, some positive and some negative. We can change our habits of working too hard or failing to delegate in our personal or professional lives by changing the *routine* in the "cue–routine–reward" habit loop. What this means is that we can't readily change a bad habit, so we have to substitute a more positive habit that gets us the same reward.

> **Case Study:**
> I was working with the president of a Fortune 50 company division (equivalent to a mid-size, closely held business), who worked from six in the morning until eight at night. His wife was furious. He was at a loss as to how to get out from under the weight of his habit.
>
> We created a triage: work that he had to do personally, work that could be delegated situationally, and work that could be delegated permanently. That took an hour to decide. We then agreed that he could accomplish his personal priority from eight to six.
>
> We made a great improvement for him and his family.

Going home early (or on time) is good for your business. A major factor in business valuation is whether the management team is empowered to run the company in the owner's absence.

By increasing your discretionary time in your business, you will make the business more valuable. Next, we'll discuss other ways to boost your valuation . . . and your wealth.

Valuation: Why Strategy, Systems, and Management are More Important than EBITDA

The valuation of your company is based on three important factors:

1. How attractive you are to an ideal buyer.
2. How scalable your business model is beyond your existing market.
3. Establishing a bidding war with competing buyers.

If you are highly successful in the first two factors, you may not need the third because you may decide to keep your company, since you've now turned it into a gold mine. Or, you may seek to impose your strengths on other companies and become an acquirer. Given the low returns in the bond market and the volatile stock market, your best bet may be to position the business for sale but actually keep it much longer (Figure 8.3).

Figure 8.3 Your future options

Show me the money

First, we'll focus on maximizing the valuation of your business. Although the stock market represents someone's expectations of future earnings, your situation is much more complex, and that's a good thing. Given the huge number of baby boomer business owners who plan to retire and sell their business in the next decade, it's crucial for you to differentiate yourself in this crowded market in order to attract a buyer.

An ideal buyer is a strategic buyer with deep pockets—usually a larger competitor or even a supplier—who wants to leverage your talent, your intellectual property, and your competitive advantages into other markets. If your business has been chugging along with low or no growth, that's not very exciting to a purchaser. If you could grow your business at 30 percent, 50 percent, or much more, with the right partner and additional capital, your business will be very attractive.

Why are you selling your business?

A far too common reason for selling a business is health: the business owner is sick of the business. A purchaser doesn't want your problems and worn-out equipment and people. Focus on the positive potential.

Buyers want to dramatically increase revenues and market share. They need your proprietary processes, protectable competitive advantages, and new ways to utilize your business to generate multiples of your gross revenues. It's about the top line, not the bottom line.

The accountants and the valuators will be looking backwards at your EBITDA and historical earnings. In the worst-case scenario, a valuation based on historical earnings would be a price floor. This technique is most useful for valuation for complex tax transactions or litigation and divorce situations. *Don't use these valuation-minimizing professionals to sell your future potential.*

Wealth Building Blocks: Your future earnings potential is much more valuable and exciting to a buyer than the historical earnings.

These valuation booster concepts can be applied whether you're selling or keeping your business (Table 8.1).

Table 8.1 Valuation boosters

Valuation Factor	Valuation Booster Tips
Strategy and competitive advantage	Protect your intellectual property with patents and trademarks. Prove your strategic advantage by measuring the results that you create for your customers. Continually invest in innovation to stay ahead.
Processes	Ensure that your work processes, sales methods, and information flows are thoroughly documented to improve training, compliance, and performance. Implement flash reports to show real-time results.
Management	Create a five-year organizational chart that shows management succession, career paths, and developmental plans.
Talent	Strengthen your culture to attract and retain talent. Implement performance-based compensation to reward high performers. Formalize mentoring to transfer best practices to future leaders.
Brand	Protect your brand with trademarks. Ask your customers to strengthen your brand with testimonials, case studies, and success stories.
Revenue growth	Develop high-growth plans that show how you can achieve 200% to 500% growth.

Always hire a professional! An M&A (mergers and acquisitions) specialist or corporate banker will have the broad perspective and the network to obtain an ideal buyer. John Warrillow, author of *Built to Sell*, advises to be cautious of professionals who are only presenting your business to one of their large corporate clients. The process will take several months. Keep focused on running and growing your existing business while you go through the due diligence and negotiations.

There are two remaining factors that are more important than price. They are the following:

- Terms and Conditions: These specify all of the factors relating to your planned exit and transition, including payment terms, noncompetition, any promises made regarding employee retention, working capital adjustments, and anything else up for negotiation. Focus on your "musts" and be flexible on your "wants."
- Earn-outs: Minimize this period and minimize the impact on the price. You don't want to be carrying all of the risk while you're delegated down to an employee role and someone else has all of the control and reward.

Most business owners only sell their business once. With proper planning, you have years to build up the valuation and attractiveness of your company.

Next, we'll discuss ways of flowing wealth out of your business while you still own it.

Show Me the Money: How to Convert Business Equity into Personal Wealth

"The best advice that you ever gave us, and you've given us lots, was to set up a holding company and a family trust," said Teresa Hensrud, owner and CFO of Industrial Scale Ltd (www.industrialscale.ca). Industrial Scale was founded by Vaughn Hensrud, and then taken over by his son Dale Hensrud, who is married to Teresa. Dale and Teresa have two adult daughters, and the daughters and their husbands all are working in the business. We'll talk more about them in the family business chapter.

First, always seek professional legal and tax advice about your corporate structures, as these structures need to be created correctly so that they are bulletproof.

The basic structure looks like Figure 8.4.

Your main business is your operating company. This "OPCO" conducts business with customers and suppliers, hires employees, and conducts the day-to-day operations. This is your wealth engine. The OPCO may be owned by a holding company or "HOLDCO" that you control. It is a separate legal entity.

In many situations, it makes sense that the HOLDCO owns or holds the land and buildings that your business uses in operations. The HOLDCO can also hold cash and other investments so that these funds are protected from creditors of your OPCO.

On the top of this structure, you can have a *family trust* that owns the shares of the HOLDCO. There are different kinds of family trusts—ask a professional—and they can be very powerful in terms of reducing taxes by paying dividends to adults in lower tax brackets, for example.

Figure 8.4 Wealth building legal structure

> **Wealth Building Blocks:** Creating separate legal entities including a family trust, holding company, and operating company will allow you to *create and protect wealth while minimizing taxes.*

The key to using this structure to create wealth is to position the operating company for maximum success. In other words, don't minimize taxes in the operating company. It needs fuel to grow and it needs a healthy balance sheet to be sustainable in the long-term. As the operating company generates superior profits and is able to fund itself (with or without debt), then you can transfer surplus cash to the holding company as a dividend.

Once the holding company receives the cash dividend from the operating company, it can do any or all of the following:

- Keep the cash and invest it in securities or insurance (check with your professional advisors)
- Acquire land and buildings
- Own other long-term assets that it can rent to the operating company
- Pay a dividend up to the family trust

The family trust does not typically hold assets. It receives funds and then distributes them to its beneficiaries. It may be required to send distributions to all beneficiaries equally, similar to dividends paid to a shareholder class in a corporation. Or, it may send dividends of different amounts to different beneficiaries, at its discretion, and this is called a *discretionary trust.*

In some jurisdictions, adults may receive approximately $40,000 of dividends and pay little to no tax if they have no other income. This is a very useful method of funding your child's university education or transferring cash to them for starting their lives.

In addition to the major advantages of a proper corporate structure, you have other following options for obtaining cash from your business:

- Implement a dividend policy in which a portion of earnings are always paid to the shareholders, just like some large public companies do. This instills financial discipline in management and positions the business properly for what it is: your source of wealth.

- Hiring family members as employees. You need to pay them fair market value salaries for their time and work.
- Declaring a management bonus to yourself to top up your personal income.
- Holding official board meetings at resort locations so that you can deduct the trip as a legitimate business expense. Check with your accountant on what you can deduct.

Always work with professional advisors to create legal and tax structures that help you to create and protect wealth, not just minimize taxes. The best advisors charge for their advice and don't sell products. The worst ones give away advice for free and make commissions from selling you things: Avoid these at all costs. Make sure that they are focused on your goals. Force them to explain everything in simple language. If you can't understand it, it's not going to work.

Next, we'll focus on the important mindset issues so that you can permanently shift to an abundance mentality of wealth.

True Wealth: How to Shift—Permanently—From Survive to Thrive

Do you own a 20-year-old business that's repeated its first year of start-up 20 times, and are constantly chasing cash, customers, and talent? Or, are you on cruise control, where your money is rolling in, you can ride out any dips, and you know that you can overcome any challenge? This chapter is about solidifying you in the latter position.

It's about your mindset. You either have an abundance mindset or a poverty mindset. An abundance mindset is knowing that you can create wealth and revenues. A poverty mindset means that you think you don't have any control or choices available and that your wealth is continually at risk (which it is). Abundance is about accelerating growth and poverty is about slowing shrinkage.[4]

An abundance mindset means that you know—don't just think, but know—that you can create more revenues and more wealth (discretionary time). Business owners are very unique in that power. The fastest way to generate new revenues is to develop new products or services and

---

[4]For an entire book on this subject, see *Thrive* by Alan Weiss (Las Brisas Research Press, 2010).

offer them to your existing customers who already know you and love you. What percentage of your revenues is from offerings that didn't exist three years ago? This number should be more than 20 percent. (Even a giant such as 3M used a strategic "must" that 25 percent of revenues had to be generated by products that didn't exist five years prior. That's how you stimulate innovation.)

This is the purpose of your business strategy: to be continually innovating and developing new things that your customers are willing to buy from you rather than your competitors. One of your strategic core competences needs to be developing new ways of doing what you've always done, improving delivery, enhancing speed, making it easier for your customers to buy, and making it harder for your competitors to copy you.

> **Wealth Building Blocks:** The most powerful source of wealth is your continual persistence to offer new value in the market.

> ### Case Study: Clear Lake Lodge
> When my family owned Clear Lake Lodge in the early 1980s, interest rates were hovering around 20 percent. The accountant threw up his arms and said, "I'm amazed that you're not bankrupt." As you can tell, that wasn't useful advice!

We were all working hard and saving money to meet the payments. If we didn't meet the payments, we could lose our houses, as my parents' and my uncle's and aunt's houses were remortgaged for bank security. Clearly, this was not worth the risk. *Abundance comes from taking prudent risks where you can control the outcomes. Poverty comes from being controlled by the economy, the bank, and other external factors.* Just because the bank is willing to lend you money, this doesn't mean it's a good business strategy. It only means that the bank is well-secured.

Here are seven ways that you can thrive in your business and your life.

1. Protect and enhance your creative, entrepreneurial power by taking risks, rewarding yourself for efforts, and celebrating failures. Those failures mean that you're now even closer to the next success.

2. Create the reserves that you need to remove self-doubts. Operating businesses should have at least three months of operating cash on hand and ideally six months of cash. This cash can sit in your holding company which can make it creditor-proof from your operating company.

3. Implement a dividend policy where your operating company regularly transfers surplus cash that is not needed for growth into your holding company. This way, you can eventually become your own bank.

4. Although it may be useful to have a trusted advisor act as devil's advocate for major initiatives, don't accept any unsolicited advice, ever, from unqualified people (often family) as it's for the benefit of the giver, not you. In fact, distance yourself (permanently) from negative people who don't understand an entrepreneur's DNA. You can hear them a mile away: They talk about pensions and going home at five o'clock.

5. Make sure that your spouse supports you. If they're worried about pensions, for example, create a financial plan and build up the investments so that this topic doesn't come up any more. One business owner simply keeps a large cash balance in the house operating account and the spouse isn't worried any more.

6. Tell yourself the truth: You've made it. You're not a start-up any more. Nobody will take away your house or family.

7. Live well. Travel well. First class isn't an airline ticket, it's the mindset that you deserve to be well taken care of in everything that you do.

Once you've got the mindset to continually thrive, you're ready to take on significant challenges of succession planning and positioning your business for the future.

PART 4

Special Cases

CHAPTER 9

Succession and Transition: Why There's No Success in Succession and What to do About It

Succession planning starts in one of four places: the kitchen table, the boardroom table, the hospital emergency room, or the funeral home. The last two are not good. However, many business owners—73 percent,[1] actually—don't have a documented succession plan. They tell us that succession is about selecting one relative over another, death, and taxes, so they put off making a plan.

When public companies talk about succession, they are talking only about senior management continuation. Succession planning in privately held companies, however, is about two things: management and ownership. Both are important but they must be treated separately. Trying to do both of them at the same time complicates things unnecessarily, creates confusion and turmoil, and derails the entire process.

> **Case Study:**
>
> Knight Archer Insurance, a mid-size insurance company with six offices, planned its succession from the founders, Doug and Gloria Archer, to family ownership and leadership. James Archer, their son, was groomed to be the president and took over from his parents this year after Doug and Gloria clearly identified their exit timelines at one of their annual strategy retreats four years ago. Tracy Rogoza, their daughter, is now the executive vice president of insurance operations. Lindsey Archer, their

---

[1] PwC, 2015 U.S. Family Business Survey, http://www.pwc.com/us/en/private-company-services/publications/2015-family-business-survey.jhtml accessed on May 30, 2015.

daughter, is active at the ownership level. The company did several things right, including the following:

- Held annual strategy sessions with senior leadership and ownership that were facilitated by an external consultant
- Set timelines for Doug and Gloria to exit
- Identified roles and development opportunity for James and Tracy who were both active in the business
- Brought in their nephew, Adam Knight, a CPA, to contribute professional financial management and strengthen management
- Focused on recruiting and retaining management talent to strengthen the management team and increase capacity for long-term growth
- Focused on long-term growth through acquisition while reinvesting profits into the company
- Implemented their succession plan

Leave a Legacy or Leave a Mess: Why Owners Avoid Succession Planning and How to Get Started Today

Rob Sobey is a fourth generation Sobey family member and is one of eight governors in the 108-year-old family business, Empire Company Limited, who operate the Sobey grocery empire. Empire became a public company in 1982 and implemented proper governance procedures required to protect shareholder value and oversee corporate performance. Succession planning became the board's formal responsibility, one of their top priorities.

Rob says, "In public companies, the board's main focus is on strategy and succession of leadership. In family businesses, the leaders are very active in the day-to-day. They typically don't put succession on the front burner. Many procrastinate as they don't want the emotional shrapnel that comes with family business dynamics, succession, and choosing one family member over another. They need professional help."

Without a succession plan, business (and personal) wealth is exposed to significant risk. A lack of succession planning will result in turmoil when something happens, and something will. In this chapter, we'll discuss how to prepare your business for succession or sale.

The Succession Quiz

- What would happen to your business and your family's wealth if you died yesterday?
- Who would your spouse call to take control of your business?
- Who is next in line to run the business?
- What would happen to your shares and wealth?

Without a succession plan—and an updated will—you will be leaving a mess.

> *If your will isn't up to date, please put this book down now and call or e-mail your lawyer to set up an appointment to update your will.*

In addition to Mr. Sobey's reasons above, business owners procrastinate about succession planning because:

- Advisors tell them that they're creating succession plans *but they're really creating estate or tax plans.* Formal succession planning never gets done properly.
- Owners perceive that "thinking about" succession means that they have a plan. It doesn't.

The first step in the succession two-step process is about ownership (Figure 9.1). To get you started with a succession plan, or to update your existing plan, perform these steps *after holding the appropriate discussion with your spouse, significant other, and/or family members:*

1. Discuss your future ownership and management succession plans with your trusted business advisors.
2. Always hire an expert experienced with family businesses or trained in the complexities of privately held business succession issues. This person will quarterback the entire process and guide your accountant and lawyer as needed.

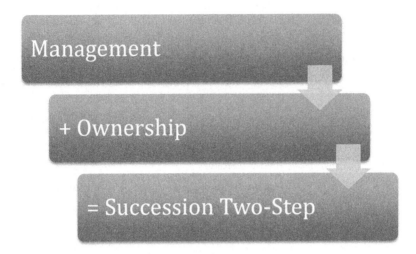

Figure 9.1 The succession two-step

3. Call your lawyer and ask them to review your corporate minute books and ensure all filings are current. This should be done annually.

4. Ask your lawyer to draw your legal structure on one page.

5. Ask your accountant to analyze your legal structure for tax efficiency, wealth protection, and flexibility to sell or transfer shares in the future. Adjust plans, structures, or shareholders proactively, that is, while you're alive and able to do so!

6. Update your wills accordingly.

Wealth Building Blocks: A succession *plan* is a document, not a discussion.

Now, let's talk about management succession.

1. Identify your current management team on an organizational chart.

2. On a future-oriented organizational chart, list who the leaders will be in five years, who requires additional training or development, and who will not make the cut (and therefore what new talent will be needed).

3. Develop plans to strengthen the keepers and fill the gaps.

4. Ensure that you have at least two and preferably three viable candidates for key positions.

5. Inform the candidates of their future potential and your expectations. That will improve retention as well.

6. Write everything down. Discuss it with your advisors and ensure that you have the corporate and management structures in place to fit your future needs.

Succession planning is simple, but it's not easy. The key is to start today. The next major step is for you to plan your own transition from management to leadership.

Be a Lobster and Shed Your Shell: Transitioning from Management to Leadership

For a lobster to grow, it must shed its old shell and then grow a new one. This process is called molting. Until the new shell solidifies, the lobster is vulnerable to predators.

As a business owner, you need to shed your management shell to become the president, a real president, who focuses on long-term, strategic issues. You will still be vulnerable to deferring back to your day-to-day role, but you must resist.

Case Study: Donna Dynna and MuniSoft

"I finally feel like a real president," exclaimed Donna Dynna. I mentioned Donna's story earlier when she was pulled out of early retirement and thrust back into management to run her company, MuniSoft, after her husband, Glenn, passed away suddenly. It took a couple of years for Donna to put her management team in place, let go of her former technical and day-to-day management roles, and focus on the future.

"At first it felt uncomfortable because I was used to working in the business and I knew what was going on. Now, I rely on my excellent management team, led by Nicole, the general manager, and our regular meetings, to keep track of progress. I can see and control where the company is going. That took some getting used to, but the future is more fun," she explained.

Wealth Building Blocks: Your optimal value is creating an ideal future state for your business, not juggling daily demands of operations and marketing.

The transition from general manager to president is not clear or easily defined. Essentially, you assign responsibility for management tasks to other people, coach and mentor them as they gain skills and confidence, allow them to make mistakes so that they learn, and eventually they will take on more and more responsibilities. This transition is a process, not an event. You will go through a similar transition to become the president. Ideally, you will also have a mentor or trusted advisor to help you become "You, President."

The day that you became the president is also the day that you should identify your successor as president (and one or two backups). Once you've become comfortable in your role as president, you can begin to mentor your future successor.

General Electric is famous for developing leadership talent. At GE, leaders and future leaders are continually identified, groomed, positioned for success (overseas assignments are common), evaluated, promoted, fired, or recruited by other companies. In fact, GE has developed more leaders who went on to become CEOs and lead other major organizations in the United States than any other single company. They have great "bench strength," and could afford to lose executives such as Larry Bossidy who went on to become a successful CEO of other companies and best-selling business author.

The three factors for growth are information, working capital, and management depth. Management, by far, is the most important factor, and the most difficult to develop, for dramatic growth. Strong managers will figure out the information and working capital requirements along the way. Developing leadership talent will accelerate your growth and build your business wealth extremely quickly because you will have the people to lead your company when it's two or three times as large.

The reason that CEOs are paid millions of dollars is because they're generally worth it: They add value to their shareholders by adding value to their customers. As a business owner, you need to position yourself to add significant value to your customers and shareholders.

Here are five steps that you can take to strengthen your leadership skills:

1.   Take an intense leadership course from an established university. These are typically one-week events and you will meet peers from across the country. (The ultimate is probably the Harvard advanced course for senior executives that runs over several weeks.)
2.   Reach out to recently retired executives who may be interested in personally mentoring or coaching you.
3.   Mentor younger managers in your organization. Teaching always strengthens your own learning and improves your skills.
4.   Read about other successful organizations and their leaders. Often, historical biographies are a better source of leadership advice than executive biographies of people who happened to be in the right place at the right time!
5.   Create an advisory board of experienced people (not your accountant or lawyer) who can advise you on your leadership development and business goals.

Shedding your management shell is scary at first, but becoming the biggest lobster in the sea definitely has its privileges. For one thing, you won't fit in most nets. Remember, you have to be vulnerable at times to grow and shed your existing limitations.

Once you've created an organization that has a strong leadership pipeline, you might decide to promote yourself to be the chairperson and keep your company running on auto pilot, or you may decide to sell.

For sale, Not Up for Grabs: Preparing Your Business for Sale

Most business owners sell their business only once. It's a huge financial and emotional transaction that requires professional help to navigate and negotiate. Preparing your business for sale includes identifying potential buyers, making your business more attractive to those buyers, and organizing your information and your company for the sale process.

If you're selling, you want to have more than one qualified buyer bidding on your company to maximize price.

> **Wealth Building Blocks:** You want to have multiple buyers interested in acquiring you in order to create a bidding war and to push up the price.

There are three kinds of buyers (Figure 9.2), and they are not all equal. A *strategic buyer* is a larger competitor or supplier who can combine your processes and market share with their processes and market share to grow quickly. They may retain some key managers but likely replace leadership positions (CEO, CFO) with their own people. Strategic buyers have the deepest pockets and can write the largest checks.

Their due diligence will be ruthless and they'll grind you on price, on terms, and on everything else. Stand firm as you likely have lots of leverage since they want you. They may require you to stay for a few years and might tie some of the purchase price to future performance, called an earn-out.

A *financial buyer* is a private equity firm that will purchase up to a majority of your shares (but probably not all of them) and load you up

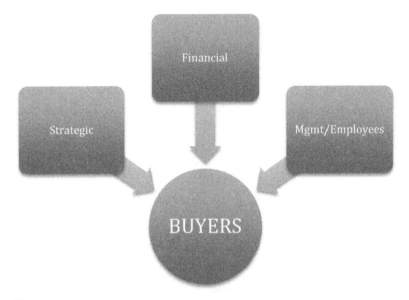

Figure 9.2 Three types of buyers

with cash and debt to fund growth. This scenario is ideal if you want a partner to support your growth while you maintain some ownership. They will likely leave management in place and take a seat on your board. They will want to exit in five to seven years at the same multiple (or higher) they bought in at originally. This can create a new problem for you in the future if you still own part of the company because you will need to find a new partner to take out the old one. You will need to fund their exit by financing or selling part of your company again.

A *management buyout or sale to family members* is the third type of buyer and we'll discuss this later.

The overall process of selling your business can be lengthy (and emotional), so you must plan ahead. You should constantly be preparing your business for sale by maximizing growth and profits, strengthening your brand and management team, and searching for buyers. If you're doing these things, your business will be in peak shape. This is the best way—by planning ahead—to improve the "Ps, Ts, and Cs" (price, terms, and conditions) to get the best deal, not just the highest price.

Preparing for a sale

The overall process of preparing for a sale and making your business as attractive as possible to a buyer include the following major steps:

1. Set an exit date. You can begin courting ideal buyers early. Take advantage of market conditions and sell during boom times because booms don't last forever.
2. Analyze your tax situation and alternatives.
3. Identify an ideal buyer, and preferably more than one, so that you can create a competitive bidding situation. A mergers and acquisitions specialist can identify multiple buyers.
4. Continue to focus on growth of revenues, profits, and cash flow. Buyers are investing in your future cash flows; keep trending up.
5. Enhance your brand, market share, product/service offerings, and momentum. These will be highly attractive to a strategic buyer. The worst thing you can do is to go into cruise control mode, reduce some expenses, and artificially boost profits.
6. Start building your information data bank. Due diligence can be a major distraction if your information isn't organized. Include

sales trends and margins by product, customer, and location. Customer and supplier contracts are golden.

7. Write your own annual reports. These capture what happened last year, strategic initiatives, risk management, leadership, and succession. These become your corporate history. All businesses should do this every year.

8. Build your team of professionals including tax, legal, and a transaction specialist. Always seek professional advice.

You need professional help to convert your years of sweat equity into cold, hard cash. Now that you've positioned your company for a sale, we'll discuss how to find buyers and negotiate the sale.

Foxtrot, Waltz, or Tango: Negotiating the Sale

Selling your business isn't just about getting the right price. There are many important variables that must meet your needs and align with the purchaser's needs. These require communication and negotiation.

Your company was built over decades, perhaps over generations. Your DNA is in your company. Owners want to protect what they've built, sometimes to a fault. What are your "must haves" from selling your business?

The most common negotiation factors include the following:

1. Sale of assets or shares
2. Retaining employees
3. Head office location
4. Company name
5. Community involvement
6. Length of time for the principal to stay on
7. Purchase price
8. Timing
9. Form of payment

The entire deal structure will need to be discussed and agreed upon prior to the Letter of Intent (LOI) being issued by the purchaser.

> ### Success Story
>
> Finning International Inc. is the largest Caterpillar heavy equipment dealer in the world. On May 6, 2015, Finning announced an agreement to acquire the operating assets of Kramer Ltd, a third generation, family-owned Caterpillar dealer based in Regina, Canada, for the sum of 230 million dollars (Canadian). According to an article in the Regina Leader Post,[2] Tim Kramer, the president of Kramer Ltd, stated "When we started this whole deal, the first (item) on the table was job security for my people. . ."
>
> Mr. Kramer sought long-term job security for the valued employees that helped his family build their business. He made his "must haves" known to the buyer right from the start of the negotiations.

Negotiations are ultimately about both parties communicating.

> **Wealth Building Blocks:** The starting point of any negotiation is to be very clear on what you *must* achieve from the sale.

Next, finding buyers can be as simple as approaching a much larger competitor and asking them to acquire you. However, this will not create a scenario of multiple buyers and will likely result in a lower price. You will increase the probability and size of a successful transaction by hiring a professional who specializes in selling businesses. They will know companies interested in growing through acquisition and can create a competitive situation.

Once you've found potential buyers, the dance begins. It's very important to maintain confidentiality and discretion during this process. You want to keep things stable, preserve customer relationships, and retain key employees (often a necessity for the buyer) during these very early and preliminary stages.

First, you will require the potential acquirer to sign a confidentiality and nondisclosure agreement. Then, you will provide them with a Confidential Information Memorandum that includes high-level information such as historical financial statements, tax returns, revenue trends, management organizational chart, and a partial customer list.

---

[2]http://www.leaderpost.com/business/Kramer+acquired+Finning/11035968/story.html accessed on May 24, 2015.

You want to assess the buyer's seriousness and qualifications as well, during this process. Over time, as you become more comfortable with the buyers, you will provide them with increasingly relevant and important information, so they increase their interest in acquiring you.

The buyer is attempting to build their case for acquiring your company. They need all relevant information, good and bad, to determine what they will offer to you in a LOI. The LOI needs to meet both the buyer's needs and your needs as the seller.

You need to provide them with factual (positive and negative) information so they can make an accurate assessment. If the buyer discovers important negative information during their due diligence that you did not advise them about, they will lose their trust in you and be concerned about more hidden surprises.

When the buyer is satisfied with the preliminary information, they will draft the LOI outlining the deal structure, terms, conditions, price, and expectations. Ideally, you will have more than one buyer analyzing your high-level information so that you can receive multiple LOIs. You can counter the terms of the LOI.

When you accept and sign the LOI, the buyer will have exclusivity and you can't accept another Letter of Intent. The buyer will commence detailed due diligence. If the buyer finds any surprises during due diligence, they can potentially reduce the price (or get scared off).

Larger companies that have grown through acquisition often have their own professionals on staff to conduct these transactions. You don't. In other words, don't bring a knife to a gunfight. Protect yourself by working with professionals and focusing on your goals.

Once you've sold your business, you're ready to ride off in the sunset, unless you've sold to your family. We'll discuss family businesses next.

All in the Family: Transitioning to the Next Generation

Ewen and Shirley Morrison went from the kitchen table to the boardroom table when they invited 15 employees and managers, including several family members, into ownership of the company that they had founded, EMW Industrial Ltd. This was a transition of both management and ownership.

Here is how Ewen describes the transition: "EMW helps international agribusiness, food production, and mining companies to maintain and improve their production with our industrial maintenance and construction services. Our large customers like Cargill, Richardson Pioneer, Mosaic Potash, and Potash Corporation of Saskatchewan kept asking me to put a succession plan in place. As our company grew, we did more work for our customers, and we became more important to their overall operations. They wanted to make sure that my company could continue if I got hit by a beer truck."

"We needed to expand both management and ownership to ensure that the company had the talent and resources to continue. This also created a transition plan for Shirley and me to eventually exit the company. We carefully evaluated our employee and management group and decided to invite 15 people into ownership. We made tough choices and there were some hard feelings. A few people left. But I had to do what was best for the company, said Ewen."

> **Wealth Building Blocks:** A management or family transition to ownership requires patience, clear and open communication, and, most importantly, a common vision.

The transition process

These are the major steps required to achieve ownership and management transition.

1. Create an advisory team consisting of you, a succession planning quarterback, lawyer, and accountant, who help you evaluate the options.
2. Decide on the general structures for ownership and management.
3. Identify potential leaders and contributors.
4. Prioritize this list, evaluate, and select the successors.
5. Meet with the selected successors individually to present the offer.
6. Give everyone time to evaluate the offer, meet with their own advisors, and discuss with their family.

7. As a group, and with the advisors, create the Unanimous Shareholders' Agreement (U.S.A.) that outlines the buy-in, governance, structure, terms, and conditions.

8. Finalize the U.S.A. (this process took several months). Have everyone sign the agreement and send their share purchase money to the lawyer.

9. Professionalize management and ownership with clear goals that focus on results, training, information, and regular meetings to create accountability.

The pros and cons of selling to family or management

There are several advantages that may help to offset the lower price or the slower payment terms, including:

- You are familiar with them and know their values, strengths, and weaknesses.
- They already know your customers, suppliers, and how things work.
- This allows your family to retain ownership.
- This can perpetuate your legacy.

The disadvantages include:

- This transition is usually gradual so you'll need to stay involved.
- Management and family typically don't have deep pockets so you won't get a large payment unless they obtain financing.
- New owners want more decision-making power. You may give up control even though you haven't been paid out yet.
- The new owners usually want to grow the business and reinvest profits. This will conflict with getting your money out quickly.

A management or family transition can help you leave a legacy and reward those who built your business. The key is maintaining control and influence so you get paid. Holding debt that can be converted back to equity gives you that power.

This is a good time to summarize some of the earlier points in conjunction with the consideration of a sale to family or management.

To make a sale attractive, the business must have significant worth (valuation) which can't be created a month or even a year prior to such a sale. It must be started *now*, even if you have no immediate sales plan. That's because high worth takes time to develop and is even more impressive when sustained over time. You're asking people to take a risk in the purchase of your business, so it's better to show a *prudent risk* with a high-value company rather than a dangerous gamble with an erratic one.

You'll also want to create a self-sustaining operation, so that your presence is not required. You need the option to hand over the keys and walk away (and, often, for someone to demand you hand over the keys and walk away to ensure your fingers are off the controls). This requires that you would have delegated key decision making and provided autonomy to appropriate people.

Finally, you want an employee force loyal to the company, not solely to you. One of the great assets and worth is a low-attrition, highly committed labor force that will serve the new ownership well, retaining key clients, suppliers, and other vital ties.

Now, if you've transitioned to your family, there are many special dynamics to consider, and we'll discuss these in the next chapter.

CHAPTER 10

Family Business: Why You Shouldn't get Business Advice at the Dinner Table

The purpose of your business is to feed your family. And that's exactly why you shouldn't get business advice at the dinner table: The family has a huge conflict of interest.

As a corporate director, *"you have a fiduciary duty to manage the business according to what's in the best interests of the corporation, not the family,"* says Rob Sobey. When you bring family into the decision-making process, emotions and relationships can trump logic and profits. You've probably already seen this happen on some occasions.

Managing the family dynamics of a family business is not only difficult, it is also crucial, to protect your wealth. Huge family blowups have resulted in the losses of millions of equity, and even the entire family business, for large families like the McCain's, Eaton's, and the horror story of the Pritzkers, who had to break up the Hyatt Hotel empire to satisfy feuds, suits, ego, and tens of millions in legal fees.

Getting Governance Right: How to Shift from the Kitchen Table to the Boardroom Table

Do you run your business like you run your family? Or, do you run your family like you run your business? Although there is no single, perfect way to manage a family business, we've seen many things that work and more that don't. Sooner or later, your board or your management team will grow, or have already grown, beyond the number of chairs that you have at your kitchen table. It's time to get "corporate," and move everyone into the boardroom.

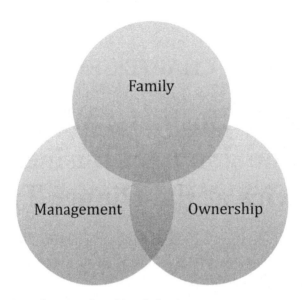

Figure 10.1 Three circles of family business

In any family business, there are three main groups: family, owner-ship, and management. This is based on the popular "Three Circle Model of Family Business" that was originally created by R. Tagiuri and John A. Davis. Our version looks like Figure 10.1, as we put the family on top so that the business reports to, and supports, the family.

Each of the groups requires its own governance structure, set of plans, and performance metrics.

Let's start with the family. The family will include people who may or may not be owners, managers, employees, or a combination of those roles. The family members who don't work in the business continually tell us that they're tired of all of the shoptalk at the dinner table. *A good rule is to focus on the family, not the business, at the dinner table.*

The best governance model for a family is called a family council, where appointed individuals from different generations focus on putting the family first. The family council creates and protects family traditions, organizes important events, and distributes relevant business information to keep family members appropriately informed. The plan can include an annual calendar of events, vacations, and even a family retreat that cele-brates accomplishments and provides personal developmental opportuni-ties. If you've ever missed your child's birthday or school performance because of work, you know that this is simple but not easy.

The governance form of management comprises the management or executive team. Their role is to implement the board's strategic plan, develop an operational plan and metrics, and execute the strategy.

The ownership's governance model is a board of directors. Smaller family businesses often don't formalize the board, and they should. An alternative is to develop an advisory board that can provide guidance and share experiences with the owners. The formal plans include a strategic plan for the company's future growth and a succession plan for both leadership and ownership. The metrics include overall business performance, valuation, cash flow, and ensuring that the strategic and succession plans are written down and updated regularly. Are your strategic, succession, and business plans written down, reviewed regularly, and amended as conditions dictate?

Wealth Building Blocks: The lack of a formal board of directors or advisory board is hurting your leadership, business performance, valuation, and net worth.

Effective governance of the family, management, and ownership will enable you to position the business for continual and sustainable growth.

Stewardship: Are You Building an Annuity or Draining the Tank?

Stewardship is about building a profitable and sustainable business that will not only support you and future generations of owners, but will also thrive in any economy. It's about reinvestment, reserves, and rewards (Figure 10.2).

The first step in stewardship is reinvestment in your company, your people, your capacity, and your brand. It's foregoing short-term gratification and then applying energy and money to create a stronger future. Family businesses are much better at this than publicly traded companies that are chasing their quarterly share prices. What is your reinvestment policy?

Reserves give family businesses the peace of mind that they can ride out the next business cycle. They show up on your balance sheet as high cash and low debt. How strong are your reserves?

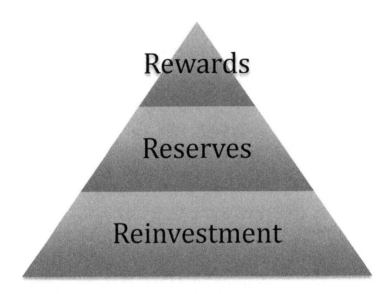

Figure 10.2 The stewardship pyramid

The third part of stewardship is rewards. These aren't just financial, as reinvestment will often dictate how financial surpluses are best used. Rewards are the control and confidence that you have over the future strategic direction of your company, its ownership and management, and its ability to overcome future setbacks.

If you take the rewards out of your company as soon as the profits are generated, then you won't have funds for reinvestment or reserves. That will put your company at risk and reduce your long-term wealth. It depends on your age, your personal financial goals, and the needs of your company.

Wealth Building Blocks: Reinvesting in your own business can generate the highest financial returns because you control how the funds are used to create more success.

If you are planning on selling some of your shares to family members and want to take advantage of any capital gains exemptions, make sure that you seek professional advice so that your company's shares qualify for the exemption. You might need to move cash out of your operating company and into your holding company to keep your operating company pure for the exemption.

Mother Parkers Tea and Coffee is the fourth largest coffee roaster in North America. The company provides coffee to McDonalds, Tim Hortons, and many other restaurants and grocery stores. This third generation family business is led by co-chief executives, and brothers, Michael Higgins and Paul Higgins Jr. They kept their dividends (rewards) modest. They reinvested in technology, increased capacity, and improved efficiencies.

Dean Robinson is the managing partner of Redmans, a business advisory and accounting firm in Narellan, New South Wales, near Sydney, Australia. From his two decades of advising families in business, he says that, "The best family businesses focus on three key factors for stewardship: destination, direction, and debris. They have a very clear view of their future destination in terms of what they do and don't do, their product and service offerings, their target clients, and their delivery processes. Next, they have clear directions and a roadmap on how to execute their strategies, how to measure progress, and how to get back on track when necessary. Finally, they have a plan to reduce or eliminate the debris, overcome obstacles, and even deal with rogue family members who won't support the destination or direction."

One industry that has historically been strong at stewardship is agriculture. Kim Gerencser, president of K.Ag Growing Farm Profits Inc., says that many family farms have been built on the concept of stewardship. "Farmers have always dealt with the weather, global prices, and many risks that other businesses don't face. A bad crop two or three years in a row could wipe them out. They've had to build up their own reserves so that they could survive tough times and retain ownership for future generations. Now, farms are much larger, and the best ones operate with a corporate mindset, with business plans, cost management, and science. That's the key to stewardship for farming families," he says.

Reinvesting in your company and building reserves will:

- increase the value of your business,
- enhance the financial performance, and
- make it more attractive to an investor such as a family member or a third-party acquirer.

Now that we've built up the family business for long-term success, it's time to determine who the boss really is.

Who's the Boss? Keeping Business First and Family Second at the Office (and the Opposite at Home)

Who was the best boss that you ever had? Why?

When Geoff Molson first graduated from university, he asked his father, the president of Molson Brewing in Canada at the time, for a job. "Son, we'll hire you when we see value in you," was his father's response, according to Geoff, who told this story at the Canadian Association of Family Enterprise chapter gala dinner a few years ago.

Geoff went on to work at other large companies in finance, obtaining promotions, building up his skills and experience, and eventually impressing his father enough to get hired. Recently, Geoff, a seventh-generation Molson family member, was appointed chairman[1] of Molson Coors Brewing Company, a global corporation formed from the 2005 merger[2] of Coors and Molson.

> **Wealth Building Blocks:** Family members should be hired *only* when they are the best candidates for the position.

The business boss has a fiduciary duty to do what is best for the company. Rob Sobey says that the business must come first, and that family comes second. If the business isn't healthy, it can't support the family. How do you run your family business: like a business or like a family?

The best hiring practices in family business today require family members to:

- obtain formal education,
- work at least five years in a large, nonfamily business, to gain corporate experience,
- achieve at least two promotions in the corporate world, and
- be the best candidate for the position.

---

[1]http://www.businesswire.com/news/home/20150603005341/en/Geoff-E.-Molson-Succeeds-Peter-H.-Coors#.VXNuwOc6d1M accessed June 6, 2015.
[2]http://www.bizjournals.com/denver/stories/2009/12/21/daily45.html accessed June 6, 2015.

The worst family business practices include the following:

- Telling family members that you will always have a place for them, thus creating a fallback position.
- Having parents directly supervising their children.
- Employing family members just because they're family and without regard to skills or performance.
- Failing to have formal performance reviews done on family members by nonfamily managers.
- Employing family members who are otherwise unemployable and not valuable to your company. (If you choose to support someone because they can't support themselves, do it with after-tax dollars and outside of your corporation. Otherwise, you're creating a culture of entitlement and your peak performers will leave for more positive cultures.)

Take an inventory of all of your employees and compare family members to nonfamily employees (Figure 10.3). What are your performance standards? How do you develop and reward your employees? What message are you sending to your employees about performance? What culture have you created for your company?

Figure 10.3 Criteria for hiring and promotion

In some of the best-run family businesses that we've worked with, the family members are held to a higher level of performance and accountability than nonfamily members. The family members are called in for weekend work, take the longer shifts, and work on the more difficult projects. They lead from the front and earn the respect of everyone: other employees, customers, and suppliers.

Sometimes, you don't have family members who are ready to take on leadership roles in your company. In this case, companies will hire professional managers to execute the board's strategy and groom the incoming leaders. As your business become larger, professional management is a key part of sustainable growth. You always want the best talent that you can find, whether they're family members or not.

Keeping the family humming at home involves several simple (but not easy) habits:

- Limiting business discussions to certain times or locations, otherwise the business topics may dominate everything and alienate certain family members who don't work in the business. Besides, everyone needs a real break—every day— from the workplace.
- Prioritizing family members and family events.
- Keeping family members who don't work in the business apprised of important events in a structured way, such as through a family council.
- Supporting all family members in their personal pursuits and interests.
- Treating all family members equally at home and not based on their position in the family business.

Who's the boss? The business should be the boss at work. The family should be the boss at home.

Sometimes, though, the boss may stay in that position too long. We'll present solutions to this next.

Dear Mom and Dad: You're Fired!

Prince Charles of Britain, at age 66, should already be retired. He's not. In fact, he's still waiting for his dream job of being King of England if his mother, Queen Elizabeth II, ever steps down. At this writing, at the age of 89, the Queen is still going strong and has no plans of retiring in the near future. The Queen's mother lived to be 101 years old, so Charles may have to keep waiting.

Is the path to the top a royal pain in your family business or are the leaders hanging on because the next leaders aren't ready yet?

The Royal Family is not alone in the longevity of their leaders. We've met, seen, or heard about leaders who are still making valuable contributions in their senior years. What's in the best interest of your business, your family, and your successors?

Stability at the top is not necessarily a bad thing. According to an article in Forbes,[3] the average tenure of a public company CEO is six years, while the tenure of a family business CEO is more than 20 years. There are other significant differences in philosophy and goals of public companies compared to family businesses, as shown in Table 10.1.

However, leaders who won't let go, are past their prime, or who have their personal interests ahead of the family business create risks to the business and their wealth. Is it time for your leaders to move on? Answer these questions:

- How is the leader driving progress and new growth?
- Is the business primarily a source of dividends for the owner?
- How is the business focusing on innovation and growth?
- Is the business investing in new technology and becoming more competitive, efficient, and cost-effective?
- Is the business more attractive or less attractive to a potential investor?
- Who is the next successor and how are they being groomed for leadership? If there isn't one, that's a major problem.

As Machiavelli implies, "Power is seized, not given." You have two options to seize power: a friendly takeover or a hostile takeover.

---

[3]http://www.forbes.com/sites/ey/2014/05/06/succession-planning-is-your-family-business-parachute/ accessed on June 7, 2015

Table 10.1 Leadership factors in public companies and family businesses

Leadership Factors	Public Companies	Family Businesses
Philosophy	Aggressive	Conservative
Values	Corporate	Based on the family
Economic Driver	Quarterly performance	Protecting value, stable returns, minimal debt
CEO Focus	Short-term growth, share price	Strategic growth in the long-term
CEO Tenure[4]	Average: six years	Average: 20 years or more
Succession	Formalized: it's the board's responsibility	Informal, emotional, creates risk to wealth

At Industrial Scale Ltd, a friendly takeover is underway. Dale and Teresa Hensrud are the second-generation owners of the company founded by Dale's father, Vaughn Hensrud. The company's growth was driven by their continual focus on quality, including ISO 9001 certification around 2001. The Hensrud's two daughters, Kristin and Brittany, and their husbands, Rae Torrie and Justin Brotzel, all work in the family business and have participated in CAFE.[5] The kids had a plan. One day, Dale and Teresa were approached by their youngest daughter, Brittany: "Mom, Dad, what are your plans for the business? What are our roles in the business in the future?"

That conversation commenced an ownership transition plan with the help of their financial advisor, lawyer, and accountant.

Wealth Building Blocks: The best way to acquire the family jewels is to earn your parents' trust and respect by working in the business. Then, commence a friendly takeover that is in their—and your—best interests. The key is communication.

The keys to avoiding a hostile takeover are for the upcoming leaders to demonstrate competence and initiative, just like Brittany and Kristin did.

---

[4]Ibid.
[5]The family members are active in the Canadian Association of Family Enterprises (CAFE), including the Personal Advisory Groups, where they get peer support for family business topics, such as succession planning.

This will take courage to open up the initial conversation. It also helps if your family business develops a formal succession plan. The Royal Family's succession process dates back to the 17th Century[6] and even involves Parliament, but yours doesn't need to be quite as formal.

It's also important for the outgoing leaders to have other roles and hobbies so that they can contribute and stay active. These can include mentoring other entrepreneurs, philanthropy, or actively supporting other organizations.

Sometimes, the leaders don't leave because the followers aren't ready to lead and the leaders don't want to put the business—and their wealth—at risk.

If you're seriously considering how to fire mom and dad, first you should look at yourself and determine how you can step up.

Dear Son and Daughter: Please Step Up!

When my family owned Clear Lake Lodge, I was left in charge one weekend. A middle-aged and well-dressed gentleman walked in, looked at our quaint lobby (this was before the Internet existed), and asked, "Do you have any rooms for tonight?" Since this was preseason, we had many rooms available. "Let me show you some of our rooms," I replied, and off we went on a quick tour.

"It's very nice," he said, "but not quite what I'm looking for."

"Why don't you stay the night, and if you don't have a pleasant stay and a great sleep, there is no charge," I offered. He laughed, accepted the deal, slept well, paid, and began bringing his wife and other guests for several years thereafter.

I knew the lifetime value of a guest was likely four annual stays of one week each, plus referrals. The cost of turning over the room was half an hour of staff time and they weren't busy anyway.

My boss, Uncle Peter, was shocked that I almost gave a room away for free but was pleased that we obtained a new customer.

As a business owner, have you let your kids run part or all of the business? Did you leave them with specific rules and checklists or were

---

[6]http://www.royal.gov.uk/ThecurrentRoyalFamily/Successionandprecedence/Succession/Overview.aspx accessed June 7, 2015

they able to use their judgment and creativity? Are you letting them make their own mistakes and learn, just like you did?

> **Wealth Building Blocks:** Stepping up means having the drive and willingness to take on responsibility, make mistakes, learn, and grow.

We can take lessons from Mother Nature. In our yard, we have several bird feeders, and some birds take up residence nearby. Mourning doves built a nest above our barbeque, right on our deck. One day, a baby bird was floundering about on the deck, under the watchful eye of our calm canine Chief Morale Officer, Lola. It wasn't flying yet, but it was ejected from the nest because it was taking up too much room and not adding enough value. Does this sound familiar?

Here are some safe ways to eject your children from the nest and ensure that they're ready to step up in the future.

- Require them to take formal education such as a university education, trades certification, or both.
- Ensure they obtain relevant working experience in a large, nonfamily-owned business so that they see how corporations work, with accountability, budgets, performance targets, and competition.
- Wait until they achieve success in the corporate world with at least two promotions and supervision of others before allowing them to join the family business.

This will give them a sense of achievement and self-worth. Education and experience assist people in achieving individuation. All adults need to shed their family labels (the "baby" of the family). Once they've become themselves, they'll be more valuable to your business, and happier to themselves (Figure 10.4).

If you're an adult child already working in the family business and you didn't have the opportunity for formal education or external experience, here are things that you can do to step up.

- Find a mentor outside of your family business who can advise you on management and business.

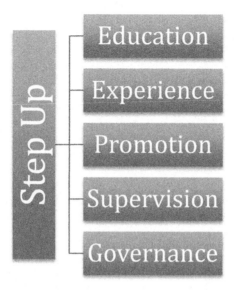

Figure 10.4 Steps to "step up"

- Take night classes at your local college in operations, marketing, sales, human resource, and finance.
- Enroll in an executive MBA program where you attend classes on alternating weekends. You will meet a great group of people, build new friendships, and expand your network.
- Gain experience working in all areas of your family business so that you will understand the business more thoroughly.
- Take short sabbaticals to work at other organizations.

One of the most important ways for all family business members to contribute is by strengthening governance. They should volunteer on the boards of local community organizations such as the food bank, learn about governance, and make contributions to others.

Stepping up requires the parents to give their children space to grow by tossing them out of the nest. It requires kids to grow by flapping their wings in education and working elsewhere.

Next, we'll discuss how business leaders and owners can apply the concepts discussed in this book and become their own consultants.

CHAPTER 11

Advising Small and Medium Enterprises (SMEs): How to be Your Own Consultant

The best consultants help you to clarify your goals, and then work backwards from your goals so that you achieve success as quickly as possible. Success is all about speed and leverage.

Conversely, beware of the consultants who rely on their methodology and checklists, charge by the hour, and can't quantify the results that they generate for their clients. You need to focus on quantifiable results such as revenues, profit, cash flow, market share, new customers, speed, proactivity vs. reactivity, and recurring business.

If you want to be your own consultant, then you need to focus on the goals and results—tangible business outcomes—that matter the most to your business. To set powerful goals, don't aim for incremental improvement of 5 or 10 percent. Aim for huge improvement such as 300 percent growth. That way, you'll be thinking much bigger, and that's the best way to create dramatic results. What's your potential?

Randy Gage, author of *Risky is the new Safe* and *Why You're Sick, Dumb, and Broke*, spoke at Alan Weiss's *Thought* Leadership Conference and said, "If you ask the wrong question, the answer doesn't matter. You have to ask the right question."

> **Wealth Building Blocks:** Being a consultant is about asking the right questions.

This chapter will provide you with the right questions to ask yourself, your family, and your management team, so that you can build your wealth and your life.

Here is the model showing how to be your own consultant (Figure 11.1).

Figure 11.1 The "M5" consulting model

What's Your Purpose? Helping Business Owners
See their Value and their Future

The purpose of your business is to provide fuel for your life. When many entrepreneurs first start their businesses, they are the fuel for the business. That's backwards. If you still have that mentality, you need to change it, like changing gears in a car. Otherwise, you'll keep thinking and acting like a start-up, and you'll never get out of first gear.

Your purpose, in part, is to continually maximize the profitability and value of your business, so that it can continually provide more fuel for your life. Your ultimate purpose, and the legacy that you want to leave, is up to you.

One of my entrepreneurial heroes is Bill Ozem. He just turned 90 years old, owns a hotel, and finances numerous real-estate properties. He has employees, including some family members, who manage the business operations. His business provides fuel for his life, utilizes his talents, and continually builds his wealth. We can all learn from Mr. Ozem.

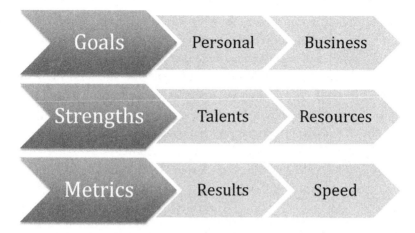

Figure 11.2 Three steps to a magnificent mindset

The process of determining your purpose and setting your mindset requires three key steps: setting the goals, leveraging your strengths and resources to accomplish the goals as quickly as possible, and calibrating your progress so that you can adjust along the way (Figure 11.2).

Purpose and mindset questions

These questions will help you to assess your mindset, set your priorities, and guide your business and personal strategies.

1. As part of your overall life plan, what are your personal goals and objectives for owning and managing your business?
2. How do you want to utilize your natural talents and passions (what you love to do) within your business?
3. In your business, how do you increase your customer's success and results? Note: Quantifying your value—a universal weakness of large and small businesses—is critical to developing your strategy and growing your business.
4. What is your ideal position in the market? This ranges from commodity provider to vendor to strategic partner.
5. What *proactive* value and offerings do you need to create and strengthen your strategic position?
6. What would your business need to look like to be 5 or 10 times as large? Creating the mindset and infrastructure for a much larger size will help you to avoid the problems of incremental growth.

7. What is your optimal business strategy in terms of your value proposition, offerings, target market, brand position, revenue goals, and organizational structure?

8. Personally, where do you want to live, how much do you want to work, and in what ways do you want to contribute and support your family?

9. What is your optimal personal strategy to help you accomplish your lifestyle goals identified in No. 1 above?

10. What are the metrics to track your "Health and Wealth" of your business and yourself?

For an electronic copy of all of the questions in this chapter, go to our special website page at http://www.symcoandco.com/resources/bwb

Spending the time to seriously consider and answer these questions will give you a foundation for growing your business, your wealth, and your life.

As Albert Einstein said, "Try not to become a person of success, rather try to become a person of value."

Once you've established your mindset, clarified your purpose, and developed your business strategy, it's time to attract the ideal customers with magnificent marketing.

Marketing Matters: Why an Outsider can Sell You Better than You can Sell Yourself

I discovered for Mercedes Benz that, ironically, their best dealers weren't problem-free (which is impossible) but rather superb at solving problems quickly and smoothly with customers (which is possible).

Conversely, I've seen local car dealers spend huge sums of advertising to attract new customers who also create arguments with their existing customers over two hundred dollars of charges that might be warranty work. That's lousy marketing.

Marketing is about increasing your ideal customer's awareness of your value so that they buy from you and increase your sales. Your value resides in your ability to make your customer—retail, wholesale, or corporate—happy.

Where does your revenue come from? Does most of your revenue come from repeat customers, referrals, recurring (automated sales like subscriptions), brand new customers, or from your sales force? Knowing who your best customers are, where they came from, and why they buy is key to being your own marketing consultant.

The most important information is why customers and prospects buy from you.

Most businesses do not quantify the results and economic value that they create for their customers and clients. This is especially relevant in business-to-business sales. However, your customers know the positive impact and value that you deliver, even if they (or you) don't specifically measure it. They know that you help them to increase revenues, decrease expenses, and increase their confidence that their businesses will continue to run and serve their customers. That's why they can sell you better than you can sell yourself.

Wealth Building Blocks: Quantifying the results that you deliver will turbocharge customer loyalty, repeat business, referrals, marketing power, and sales growth.

The best way to quantify your results is to measure your customer's performance. You need to take a scientific approach to determining your impact by monitoring your customer's increase in sales, decrease in costs, or increase in production capacity and efficiency, for example.

One method is to build in metrics into your proposal and delivery criteria. Another way is to prepare a case study of the results. Often, even your customers will be surprised—and very pleased—at the economic impact you have on their business. This exercise will increase their loyalty and allow you to capture higher margins.

We want to be clear on definitions. Marketing is not about advertising, which is only a small part of marketing. *Marketing is about increasing the awareness of your value to your ideal clients and ensuring that they know how to access you and buy from you.*

Language and numbers are very important in marketing. Use specific statements with quantified results (Figure 11.3). For example, "Our consulting CFO helped us increase profit by 150 percent and achieve revenue growth of 377 percent" is more effective and powerful than a generic statement that says "We help businesses to grow."

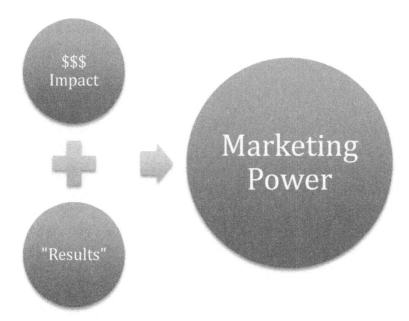

Figure 11.3 Marketing power

Marketing questions

The following marketing questions will empower you as a marketing consultant for your company.

1. Who is your ideal client, customer, or buyer? Describe them as specifically as possible.
2. What are the best methods to attract your ideal customers?
3. How do you, or can you, educate your current customers and prospects about your full range of value, products, and services to increase repeat and referral business?
4. What percentage of your revenues come from existing products, services, and customers, compared to new products, services, and customers that didn't exist three years ago?
5. How can you automate your sales (with subscriptions or automatic reorder points) to increase recurring or repeat business?
6. What percentage of your revenues and new customers comes from referrals, and how can you increase it?

7. What new offers and pricing options can you develop to allow the customer to choose their optimal investment level (that is, give you more money)?

8. How can you leverage technology and the Internet to increase your marketing reach and become a global business?

9. How often do you proactively stay in contact with your customer base and referral sources using cost-effective tools like electronic newsletters?

10. What is the most effective way to increase the market's awareness of your offerings to drive new revenue growth?

Now that you've attracted the ideal customer, it's time to deliver the goods. We'll discuss your methodologies for delivery next.

Methodology Doesn't Matter: Why Your Customers Should Never See the Engine Room

At my favorite restaurant, The Diplomat Steakhouse, they serve fantastic steaks and lamb, have an excellent wine list, and the Manhattans are always ice-cold and perfect. It's the only place in town where you can still have a Caesar salad made at your table. It's where we celebrate all our special events and where I bring out-of-town clients for a special dinner. The owners, Dimitri, Peter, and their father, John Makris, take great care of all of their guests.

I haven't been in the kitchen to see the flow or layout. How they coordinate the hustle and bustle of cooking and plating so that everything arrives hot and delicious, at the same time, is magic.

Does your company provide a magical experience for your customers? Does everything show up on time, as promised, and ready to go? Do you measure your order success rate and your customer satisfaction? If you want to be your own methodology consultant, you need to see your business from your customer's eyes.

Your methodology includes your internal processes that most of your customers will never see, although they experience it, directly or indirectly. These include internal processes such as ordering, coordinating, scheduling, project planning, and manufacturing. They also include your customer interactions including quoting, negotiating, listening, order taking, delivering, installing, testing, commissioning, invoicing, payment processing, problem solving, and after-sales servicing.

Do you have documented procedures and performance metrics for everything, or at least for the most important things?

In the restaurant industry, many franchise restaurants are more profitable than other fast food restaurants because of three factors: national marketing, information systems that record everything, and standardized policies and procedures.

When you combine the passion and talent that the Makris family has for fine dining with the discipline of documented procedures and information systems that generate timely metrics, you've got the recipe for a great business (Figure 11.4).

Case Study:
One professional services firm estimates that it can improve overall productivity and speed between 10% and 30% by designing and implementing Standard Operating Procedures for its professional staff. The gains are from identifying, codifying, and sharing internal best practices that exist in every business but are often invisible. Now, everyone can learn faster and produce better results. That's a fantastic return with no capital expenditure.

An extremely powerful way to quickly grow your business, increase your capacity without significant capital expenditure, and improve the speed and quality of your output is by getting critical information out of everyone's heads and onto paper (or computer).

Wealth Building Blocks: Document your policies, procedures, best practices, and performance standards. *Take videos of how things are done.* Have front-line people set the standards.

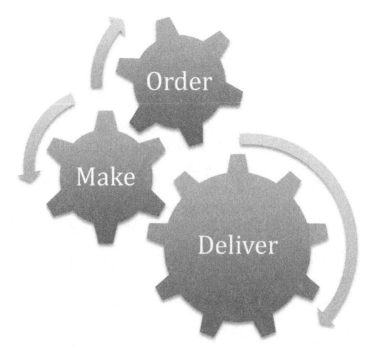

Figure 11.4 The methodology steps

Methodology questions

These questions will assess your current methodology and identify where you need to focus to improve your production.

1. How do you set your daily priorities and measure progress on them?
2. As per operational expert Rick Pay: What is your "shipped-on-time" percentage?
3. What is your current operational capacity: units produced, customers served, hours billed, or your production?
4. What processes, systems, policies, and procedures are used to ensure that you deliver a quality product—consistently and quickly—to your customers? Which processes need to be formalized?
5. How do you codify and share internal best practices to enhance your own and your team's skills, capacity, speed, and performance?

6. How long does it take your customer to place an order, beginning from when they first contact you until a contract is signed?

7. How long does it take your company to produce and deliver the customer's order, from when the order is received until it's installed?

8. How long does it take you to issue an invoice, wait for payment, and then get paid by your customer?

9. How can you accelerate each of the processes in Questions 7 through 10 above?

10. How can you increase your capacity by 20% to 40% or more without any additional Capital Expenditure (CapEx)?

Methodology is the important, but perhaps invisible, part of your business—the engine room—that can generate significant excitement for your customers and super profits for you when it's well-tuned and focused on speed.

Now that we've got your engine humming, let's focus on monetizing your transactions and relationships.

Monetization: How to Ask for, Get, and Keep What You've Earned

A few years ago, service company in high-growth mode was very busy, but they weren't making much profit, and cash flow was always tight. The problem was that they were still thinking like a start-up business, were pricing their services against other start-ups, and were letting their customers dictate all the terms. The customers were holding the company back. Who or what is controlling you?

When the company assessed its strategy, it discovered its true value to its customers. Then, it took a brave step forward and negotiated with those customers, explaining how the customers would be better off under the new business model and by paying higher fees. After some resistance, customers realized the company wasn't going to serve them under the old terms. The new model was aligned with their goals so they gradually accepted. You need to say "No!" to get ahead.

What happened after that was monetization bliss. The company effectively doubled its rates, accelerated payment terms, specified what it would and would not do, and positioned itself for success. The results were dramatic and fast. The customers loved the company's proactive focus on their results. The bankers loved management's new focus and funded future growth. The owners loved the profitable growth.

Other companies of different sizes and industries have successfully executed the same process—strategy, pricing, and speed—to achieve similar growth and success (Figure 11.5).

Monetization is about turning your strategy and value into cash. Cash flow comes from three factors: margin, velocity, and volume. While all three are important, you can control one factor more than the others.

This factor is margin.

Margin will have the largest impact on your life and your business. You can, and should, set multiple prices wherever you are able to in your business.

Pricing power depends on your brand, speed, and quality. If you quantify your economic value and the results that you create for your customers, then you will have significantly more pricing power—and marketing magnetism—than your competitors.

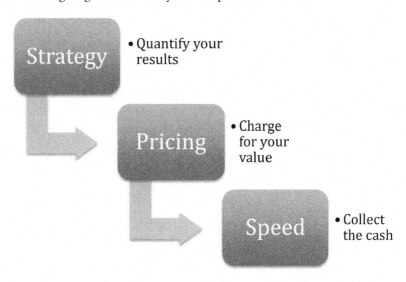

Figure 11.5 Mastering monetization

*A 10 percent increase in prices will flow directly to the bottom line as your costs haven't increase*d. If you increased top-line sales by 10 percent at a higher margin, what would your bottom line look like? That would be an impressive jump. Multiply that profit improvement by 5 to 10 times as a valuation multiple, and you've dramatically increased your business valuation (and your wealth).

How can you create pricing options for different value? For example, airlines charge more for business class or for short notice. Can you charge for speed?

This strategy will empower you to capture more margin from your customers. The worst thing that you can do in terms of pricing is to offer your customers one "take it or leave it" price. Even the local coffee shop offers different prices for different sizes of beverages.

Wealth Building Blocks: Pricing turbocharges monetization. Courage creates cash.

One other powerful method to boost monetization is leverage. Jeff Pietrobon, district director with a national financial institution, says the most important factor he considers for financing is the cash flow of the business. Strong cash flow will support financing for growth that will generate even more cash flow.

Monetization questions

You may want to send the following questions to your marketing and accounting departments and see how they respond.

1. What is the economic value of your services to your customers? This sets your strategic position in the market.
2. What value are you giving away—for free—that customers are willing to pay for?
3. What services are you providing that have high cost but that your customers don't really need or want?
4. What new value could you create and deliver that your customers would be willing to pay for?

5. What are your *Total Days to Cash*? This is about velocity. From when you pay your employees and suppliers, how long does it take until your customer pays for your final product or service?

6. Which products, services, customers, and industry segments are your most profitable and least profitable based on your "Real Profit." (Nicole Thibodeau, CPA, defines "Real Profit" as excluding arbitrary accounting allocations that distort costs.)

7. What percentage of your revenues is earned from new offerings that didn't exist three years ago?

8. If you increased production speed, how much could you increase capacity and top-line revenues?

9. How can you utilize leverage (debt) to grow your business, increase profits, and make your business more valuable?

10. What is the valuation of your business today and what could it be if you grew at 25 percent in the next year?

Reviewing these strategic and financial factors on an ongoing basis will increase your monetization and build your wealth.

So far, we've discussed your mindset, marketing, methodology, and monetization. Keeping it all together is management.

Management Magic: The Art and Science of Aligning People and Resources to Drive Results

"Most car accidents are caused because people don't look far enough ahead," according to Stéphane Langlois, a former police driving instructor. "Drivers need to look further ahead to see what's coming," he says.

It's the same in business. The manager's role is to look ahead and make decisions that create optimal outcomes for you and your customers. A professional manager focuses on the future.

Consulting to yourself on management is as simple as comparing where you are now, where you want to go, and evaluating the plans to get there, with objectivity and discipline. It's about thinking and acting like a manager.

As a manager, you need to manage your own behavior, too. That's the easiest way to influence others: leading by example.

Kelly Ozem, CPA, is my chief financial officer and business partner in Builders Group, CPAs. He's also a certified Pilates instructor and hula hoop instructor. His fitness has taught him to focus. "I have to be in the moment and focus on what I'm doing. Whether I'm preparing a complex estate plan or walking Darby (the dog), I'm only in that moment," says Kelly.

Steve McKenna, president of McKenna Distribution Ltd, a flooring materials distributor, says ". . .managing myself, my business, and my personal relationships are all related. If I'm not taking care of one of them, then all three will probably suffer."

Our basic premise is that you can grow your business and build your wealth by professionalizing management (Figure 11.6). That means:

- providing management with information and resources,
- empowering them to make decisions (hiring, firing, and spending money),
- measuring progress, and
- holding them accountable for results.

"The most important factor we use to assess a credit application is the strength of the management team," says Doug Yaremko, associate vice president at a global bank.

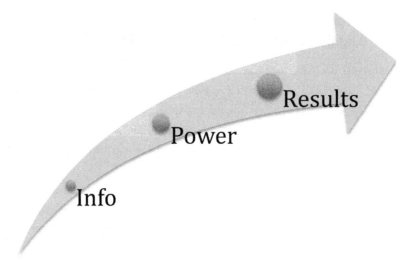

Figure 11.6 Magnifying management momentum

The major growth obstacle for many small and medium enterprises is that the founders and owners can't (or won't) let go of daily operations to focus on strategic growth. Yet, professionalizing and supporting management are the best ways to sustainable growth.

Jeffrey Scott has consulted with hundreds of landscape and building contractors across the United States. He says, "The best managed companies make sure that everyone on the team is following the same playbook." This creates capacity beyond the owner's direct involvement.

> **Wealth Building Blocks:** Sharing information is the foundation of good management. Use data, not emotions and guesses, to manage your company.

Here are some success stories of people, in progress, of pursuing growth.

Mobil Grain

"At Mobil Grain, we sell specialty crops to customers around the world. We've developed software that tracks and identifies inventory, its source, and its destination, so that our customers have real-time information on their purchases. We have total control over our processes, from order, to shipment, and payment. Our system is fully integrated," says Sheldon Affleck, owner and cofounder, along with his brother, Lavern Affleck.

RH Electric

"I started RH Electric because I was unemployed and needed to feed my family," said Randy Hrywkiw, founder of RH Electric. Today, the company is a fast-growing contractor that employs Randy's sons, Jason (the general manager), Colin, and Brock, all journeymen electricians. "I'm focused on continually improving project control so that we can allocate resources and make better decisions, faster. This makes our customers happy and us more profitable," says Jason.

Candor Engineering

Candor Engineering was acquired by Frank Shewchuk and his wife, Lana. Gilbert Chan joined ownership and became the vice president of marketing to accelerate growth. "Candor Engineering specializes in electrical engineering services for major industrial customers. We've grown dramatically by not only focusing on the engineering and design, but also focusing on providing a fantastic culture and learning/teaching environment for junior and senior engineers. Our culture definitely gives us a competitive advantage in terms of talent, capacity, retention, and customer satisfaction," says Gilbert.

Morsky Group of Companies

According to Wayne Morsky, CEO of the Morsky Group, there is a simple recipe for aligning multiple owners on growth. "First and foremost is strong and effective communication. From this, having a common goal and agreeing to the guiding principles allows the owners to move forward with continuity," says Wayne. Lorne Schnell, the President and Wayne's business partner, adds: "High growth companies are not usually going to pay out dividends because the company needs all the cash it can get to fund the growth. Frank discussions with all the owners about expectations and the need for patience are necessary."

McKenna Distribution

"Every Monday, we have a short weekly management meeting that focuses on what's coming up, any problems from last week, and what the priorities are ahead. I want everyone moving in the same direction," says Steve McKenna, president of McKenna Distribution.

MuniSoft

Donna Dynna, president of MuniSoft, brings all of her employees from across the country to attend the annual general meeting every August. "Amid friendly team-building competitions, we review what we have accomplished in the past year, and share the vision for the next year," says Donna.

Management questions

These questions are designed to increase your control while increasing your freedom from day-to-day management.

1. Are you focused on incremental growth by improving over last year, or on dramatic growth by setting huge goals and working backwards from the future?
2. What are the goals for your company, and how do you communicate these to your employees?
3. How do you measure business performance and results—sales, production, and cash flow—in real time to ensure you're on track?
4. How do you hold people accountable for results?
5. What percentage of your time is spent on administrative or operational matters compared to future strategies and growth? What should it be?
6. How strong are your professional managers in the areas of sales, marketing, operation, and finance?
7. Is your management team capable of running your business without you for two months?
8. Does your management team have a clear strategy, structured plan, and metrics to monitor their performance?
9. Do your key people have a second-in-command, or identified successor, who is being groomed for the position?
10. What does your five-year organizational chart look like, and do you have a plan to fill in the gaps?

Consulting to management requires establishing clear objectives and then evaluating alternatives that will achieve the objectives.

Always begin with the objectives, in business and in life. They have a magical way of reinforcing each other.

Conclusion

It has been our privilege to share the lessons we've learned in our consulting careers—from Wall Street to Main Street—to help you build your business wealth.

This book is built upon two business wealth building principles.

First, quantify the economic value that you provide to, and the results that you create for, your customers and clients. Leverage that powerful information to attract great customers who are willing to pay for your high value. You will dramatically increase your financial success.

Second, proactively offer to provide that value to your customers without waiting for them to place an order. This will grow your business—and your wealth—beyond your wildest dreams.

We wish you much success on your journey of being rewarded for your value, being recognized for your contributions, and sleeping more soundly because you've turned your business into a gold mine.

Thank you for your entrepreneurial spirit! It is our honor to share your journey with you.

APPENDIX

I.   Personal Balance Sheet

The Elite Owner's Personal Balance Sheet
Name: _____   **By The Business Wealth Builder®**   Date _____

> You are the economic engine for your business and for supporting your family.
> How strong is your engine? Legend: in the boxed areas, use "X" = Now; "n/a" = not applicable
> Identify and record your priorities and plans.

1 Health: your physical, mental, emotional and spiritual health are in great shape.
Strongly disagree [   ] **Strongly agree**

2 Relationships: you have a strong group of family and friends that support you.
[   ]

3 Your life partner supports you in your business, makes you smarter, stronger & more successful.
[   ]

4 Vacations: you plan ahead, take at least four to six weeks per year, feel relaxed and recharged.
[   ]

5 Time and Talent: you utilize your natural talents, are focused and productive, and enjoy free time.
[   ]

6 Net worth: you know your financial net worth, review it annually, and it is steadily increasing.
[   ]

7 Finances: are organized and structured with clear goals, you have confidence in your financial plan.
[   ]

8 Cash & Debt: you have adequate liquid investments for emergencies; any personal debt is good debt.
[   ]

9 Investments: you have quality, diversified investments that you understand & support your goals.
[   ]

10 Risks: your will & legal documents are current; you have adequate insurances to protect your family.
[   ]

11 Business Strategy: is clear & focuses your people on providing measurable value to ideal customers.
[   ]

12 Management Team: knows your goals & values, make decisions & run the business without you.
[   ]

13 Valuation: you know what your company is worth and how to maximize its valuation.
[   ]

14 Metrics: you know and receive operational, financial and qualitative information quickly.
[   ]

15 Growth: you have the resources, the plans and the people to grow significantly in the future.
[   ]

16 Talent: your people have career plans, are empowered, engaged, recognized & rewarded for results.
[   ]

17 Operations: quality and costs are in control, you can scale capacity through outsourcing or partners.
[   ]

18 Financial: working capital is a strength; capital is structured; & you pay yourself regular dividends.
[   ]

19 Exit and Risks: you have a clear exit or transition strategy and a risk management plan in place.
[   ]

20 You are having fun and sleep well at night.
[   ]

ACTION PLAN

What are your top three priorities?   Who can help you?   When?

1 _____

2 _____

3 _____

II.   Definitions

Accountant A good accountant will proactively prepare information—without being asked—to show how you can improve profits, grow your business, and maximize your after-tax cash flow so that you can build your wealth. They will not have piles of files on the floor of their office. They will meet with you before your fiscal year-end to help you plan your tax strategies. They will complete your fiscal year-end within 60 days, and ideally, within 30 days.

Accounting Department A good internal accounting department will make you money. They will improve the quality of information available to your managers so those managers can make better decisions, faster. They will balance their time among reporting on the past, the present, and the future. They will complete your month-end reports by the tenth day of the month, or even sooner, so that they can spend more time on improving future results. They will explain things in English and use charts and graphs to show important trends. They will prepare your year-end file throughout the year so that your external accountants can quickly prepare your year-end financial statements and tax returns.

Bankers A good banker will visit your operation at least annually, explain how they evaluate your business, request regular financial and management reports that demonstrate that you have control of your business, and offer total banking services that improve the growth potential of your business. They will never have the lowest interest rates but they will be competitive. They will have stability in their ranks so that you're not training a new banker every year.

EBITDA A financial term that calculates earnings before interest, taxes, depreciation, and amortization. This can be used as a quick estimate of business valuation for your internal use. For small businesses, multiply EBITDA by the multiples of three and five to show a range of valuation. For mid-market companies, multiply earnings by five to seven to show a range of valuation. There are many factors that affect the valuation multiples, so always obtain expert advice prior to buying or selling a business.

Lawyer A good lawyer will proactively recommend important legal agreements and documents that you need as a business owner to protect your business and your wealth. These include, but are not limited to, shareholder agreements, updating your wills at least every two years, power of attorney, and agreements with your key employees, customers, and suppliers. They may maintain your minute book (someone must do this annually) and ensure all annual documents are recorded and filed.

Mid-market Company A privately held entity that employs between 100 and 500 people or has annual revenues between 10 million and 500 million dollars.

Small Business A privately held entity that employs up to 100 people or has annual revenues up to 10 million dollars.

Strategy The framework that guides the intentional focus and alignment of your resources so that you can provide optimal value to your ideal customer as quickly as possible.

Succession plan In a privately held business, this involves two steps. First, all key managers need a successor identified and being developed to cover that position and to allow the incumbent to be promoted. Second, it provides for a clear transition of ownership.

Trusted Advisor An expert who proactively advises you how to achieve your goals, overcome obstacles, and remain on course, while constantly putting your self-interests ahead of his or her own.

Valuation the estimate of your business value to a potential purchaser. This may be based on earnings (see EBITDA above), cash flow, net assets, or some combination of these methods. Valuation is part art, part science, and part negotiation. Enterprise value is the valuation of your company prior to the deduction of debt.

Wealth True wealth includes discretionary time and the resources such as money and health to enjoy that free time.

Working Capital Items that consume or create cash within 12 months, including cash, accounts receivable, inventory, operating line of credit, and accounts payable. Aggressively managing your working capital can help to fund your growth.

III. Private web landing page and resources

To download free tools and access additional resources for this book, go to: www.symcoandco.com/wealthbuilder

To purchase additional copies of this book, go to: www.businesswealthbuilder.com

IV. Recommended readings

Barr, Chad and Weiss, Alan. 2012. *Million Dollar Web Presence.* Entrepreneur Press.

Duhigg, Charles. 2014. *The Power of Habit.* Random House.

Dweck, Carol. 2006. *Mindset.* Ballantine Books.

Francis, Colleen. 2014. *Nonstop Sales Boom.* Amacom.

Gage, Randy. 2012. *Risky is the New Safe.* Wiley.

Goldfayn, Alex. 2015. *The Revenue Growth Habit.* Wiley.

Goldsmith, Marshall. 2015. *Triggers.* Crown Business.

Harnish, Vern. 2014. *Scaling Up.* Gazelles, Inc.

Jantsch, John. 2011. *Duct Tape Marketing.* Thomas Nelson.

Maister, David. 2000. *True Professionalism.* Free Press.

Pink, Daniel H. 2013. *To Sell Is Human.* Riverhead Books.

Warrillow, John. 2011. *Built to Sell.* Portfolio.

Index

Join the Business Wealth Builder Community Today!

This book is only the beginning of building additional wealth in your business. There are more valuable ideas and tools at www.symcoandco.com/wealthbuilder

Continual support, community, and new ideas are the lifeblood of your future success. Some of the biggest factors in my own wealth building has been the support, fresh perspectives, new intellectual property, and experiences provided by my peers and friends. I want you to experience that environment as well.

Join me at www.symcoandco.com/wealthbuilder to see how you can:

1. **Join the exclusive Business Wealth Builder online community.** Interact with other business owners and managers who are reading the book and sharing their experiences and results. Grow along with your peers.

2. **Do your exercises.** Just like going to the gym will improve your health, doing the exercises in the book will help to improve your business. You may download PDFs of the questions and exercises in the book so that you can complete them on your computer or print them out.

3. **Download a consultant's guide.** You can integrate the content into your own business or with your clients.

4. **Access wealth building tips, newsletters, articles, videos, webinars, and proactive advice.** Wealth building is an ongoing adventure to accelerate your business growth, increase profits, and build your wealth. I will continually share new insights and advice with you on this site.

Go to www.symcoandco.com/wealthbuilder to be part of an active community that will help you to apply the concepts of the book, build your business, and create wealth.

To connect with the authors, go here:

Phil Symchych

Twitter @philsymchych

LinkedIn https://ca.linkedin.com/in/philsymchych

Blog www.symcoandco.com/blog/

Website www.symcoandco.com/

Alan Weiss

Twitter @bentleygtcspeed

LinkedIn www.linkedin.com/in/alanweissphd

Blog www.contrarianconsulting.com/

Website www.alanweiss.com/

OTHER TITLES IN THE ENTREPRENEURSHIP AND SMALL BUSINESS MANAGEMENT COLLECTION
Scott Shane, Case Western University, Editor

- *Growing Your Business: Making Human Resources Work for You* by Robert Baron
- *Managing Your Intellectual Property Assets* by Scott Shane
- *Internet Marketing for Entrepreneurs: Using Web 2.0 Strategies for Success* by Susan Payton
- *Business Plan Project: A Step-by-Step Guide to Writing a Business Plan* by David Sellars
- *Sales and Market Forecasting for Entrepreneurs* by Tim Berry
- *Strategic Planning: Fundamentals for Small Business* by Gary May
- *Starting Your Business* by Sanjyot Dunung
- *Growing Your Business* by Sanjyot Dunung
- *Understanding the Family Business* by Keanon J. Alderson
- *Launching a Business: The First 100 Days* by Bruce Barringer
- *The Manager's Guide to Building a Successful Business* by Gary W. Randazzo
- *Social Entrepreneurship: From Issue to Viable Plan* by Terri D. Barreiro and Melissa M. Stone
- *The Chinese Entrepreneurship Way: A Case Study Approach* by Julia Pérez-Cerezo
- *Enhancing the Managerial DNA of Your Small Business* by Pat Roberson-Saunders, Barron H. Harvey, Philip Fanara, Jr., Gwynette P. Lacy and Pravat Choudhury
- *Five Eyes on the Fence: Protecting the Five Core Capitals of Your Business* by Tony A. Rose
- *Hispanic–Latino Entrepreneurship: Viewpoints of Practitioners* by J. Mark Munoz and Michelle Ingram Spain
- *Open Innovation Essentials for Small and Medium Enterprises: A Guide to Help Entrepreneurs in Adopting the Open Innovation Paradigm in Their Business* by Luca Escoffier, Adriano La Vopa, Phyllis Speser and Daniel Satinsky

Announcing the Business Expert Press Digital Library
Concise e-books business students need for classroom and research

This book can also be purchased in an e-book collection by your library as

- a one-time purchase,
- that is owned forever,
- allows for simultaneous readers,
- has no restrictions on printing, and
- can be downloaded as PDFs from within the library community.

Our digital library collections are a great solution to beat the rising cost of textbooks. E-books can be loaded into their course management systems or onto students' e-book readers. The **Business Expert Press** digital libraries are very affordable, with no obligation to buy in future years. For more information, please visit **www.businessexpertpress.com/librarians**. To set up a trial in the United States, please email **sales@businessexpertpress.com**.